MARION DRAKE

# CAUGHT IN THE NARCISSISTS' WEB

*When Family Becomes The Enemy*

**DRAKE**
PUBLISHING HOUSE

*For Jordan and Nicholas*

Job 19:25-27

For I know that my redeemer liveth, and that
he shall stand at the latter day upon the earth:
And though after my skin worms destroy this
body, yet in my flesh shall I see God: Whom I
shall see for myself, and mine eyes shall behold,
and not another; though my reins be consumed
within me.

Job 38:1-4

Then the Lord answered Job out of the whirlwind...

— Job 19:25-27; Job 38: 1-4, KJV

# Contents

# Acknowledgments

First and foremost, I thank my Heavenly Father for giving me the strength to tell my story. Through every betrayal, loss, and hardship, He has been my refuge and my source of strength.

**Psalm 23**

"The Lord is my shepherd; I shall not want.

He maketh me to lie down in green pastures: He leadeth me beside the still waters.

He restoreth my soul: He leadeth me in the paths of righteousness for His name's sake.

Yea, though I walk through the valley of the shadow of death, I will fear no evil: for Thou art with me; Thy rod and Thy staff, they comfort me.

Thou preparest a table before me in the presence of mine enemies: Thou anointest my head with oil; my cup runneth over.

Surely goodness and mercy shall follow me all the days of my life: and I will dwell in the house of the Lord forever."

**Job 13:15**

"Though He slay me, yet will I trust Him."

**Don**, I am extremely grateful for your continued love and support, especially in my later years. You did not abandon me like your sisters and niece did, and for that, I am eternally thankful. Your daily texts bring me comfort, and I cherish our conversations about so many interesting things. You remain a valuable part of my life.

**Audrey**, Thank you for your love and support over the years. You have treated me far better than my own sisters ever did, and for that, I am grateful from the bottom of my heart. You, too, are a valuable part of my life. You are my true sister.

# A Letter to My Family

**To My Family,**

This book is going to be a hard read—I need to be clear about that. Within these pages, you will read about outrageous and evil acts perpetrated against children and other innocent people by some of your own relatives.

When we see evil, we must speak out. People who commit these kinds of acts rarely change and almost never take accountability.

If we stay silent, they will continue hurting others until they are firmly in their graves—because they feel untouchable. It doesn't matter how long ago it happened; the passage of time does not absolve wrongdoing, especially when there has never been accountability, remorse, or restitution.

If you ever find yourself in a similar situation, I hope you will free your soul and refuse to remain silent. Silence enables abusers. Truth exposes them. And no matter how hard the truth is to face, it is always better than living a lie.

With truth,

Marion (Poose)

# A Letter to My Betrayers

**To Sharon, Angela, Sheri, and Lance,**

Your treachery knows no bounds. You deliberately worked together—**behind my back**—with my ex-husband to take my children away. Then you **erased me** from the family and ruined my life.

You didn't just want me out of your lives—you wanted me erased **from the entire family.**

You shut me out of holidays. You shut me out of gatherings. You severed relationships that should have lasted a lifetime.

Except for Angela, **none of you have ever apologized, made amends, or tried to repair the damage.**

What you did was so despicable that **even our parents—Harry Drake and Maggie Drake—felt compelled to write damning letters about you to the court.** But that wasn't on them—they had to tell the truth.

And in the end, Harry chose me over all of you.

When it mattered most, did you really think he would do anything else? In what universe?

The man loved me more.

I am his daughter.

Get over it.

**Dr. Lance Robert,**

You married into my family, then **spearheaded a plot to destroy me**—your wife's aunt.

**You are the devil.**

You just have invisible horns.

And now, to the detriment of the public, you're teaching college and mentoring impressionable youth.

**Shame on you all.**

You rolled the dice, thinking you would win—**but the House always collects its debt.**

**—Marion (Poose)**

# Introduction

I wrote this memoir because I want my family, my friends, and all those who love me, to know what happened to me, how much I was hurt, and how much I loss.

I also wrote the book so people out there who are suffering from abuse, and who may or may not have been made the family scapegoat like I was, will realize that you deserve better, so much better. It's not your fault. There is nothing wrong with you, but there is plenty wrong with your abusers and tormentors.

There is a way out, and that is to remove yourself from the harmful environment as soon as you possibly can. You must work towards that goal diligently, and never stop until you find a way out. Your health, your happiness, and sometimes even your very life, depend upon it.

My story will unfold over the course of several books. Each book is part of a series, but each book is designed to stand alone. You won't have to wait until the last book to know the ultimate betrayal perpetrated upon me by my own family, people who were supposed to love me unconditionally, who I thought would always have my back—especially when it really mattered.

The irrefutable proof of **Sharon Malvin, Angela Malvin, Sheri Robert, and Dr. Lance Robert's** betrayal is included on my evidence page.

You will learn of all the ways they hurt me over the years, how they erased me from the family, and manipulated a court case to help my ex-husband win custody of my children—the final act of betrayal that effectively destroyed the life I had with my kids.

As my story unfolds, you will also learn how they perpetrated outrageous and evil acts against other unsuspecting, and innocent people, even their own children.

As you look back at the way they treated me over the years, you may be asking yourself how I could even trust them to begin with.

It's simple. I could never bring myself to do to somebody what they did to me. Not even to my worst enemy. So, yes, I was naive, and I thought they would never plot against me like this in the end, never destroy their own flesh and blood, their own mother's child—and in such a cruel, inhumane way.

But they did.

And they did it with the full confidence that they would get away with it.

My betrayers and abusers consistently portray themselves as kind and model citizens. They regularly attend church, and Dr. Lance Robert, a college professor, is actively involved in mentoring impressionable youth in well-known leadership organizations.

Once they blew up my life and left me wounded and bleeding in the street, they sat back, smug and righteous, and marveled at their handy work—the devil's handiwork. And they remain that way to this day—uncaring, unapologetic and sometimes even taunting.

They thought I was down for the count. They thought I was over and done with. They thought I would never recover and regain the strength I needed to tell what they had done.

They were wrong. Dead wrong.

For years, I've lived with the weight of these terrible secrets because in my family there was one sacred rule you dared not break: *Don't air the family's dirty laundry.* And for years, I complied. I didn't reveal their continued attacks, and the devastating harm they caused to my life and others.

I kept their dirty, evil secrets even though they weighed me down inside, and kept me from healing, out of loyalty to a family that was never loyal to me.

That ends now.

> *Do not go gentle into that goodnight,*
> *Rage, rage against the dying of the light.*
> — Dylan Thomas

# 1

# California's False Promises

My name is Marion, and my nightmare life began when my parents, Mag and Harry, sent me to California to live with my oldest sister, Sharon. They were losing their BBQ restaurant and house in Chicago and decided to move to California for a fresh start after the dust settled. They sent me ahead, planning to join me there in a few years after wrapping things up in Chicago and doing some traveling.

My mother had five children with her first husband, Reuben Malvin. The youngest, Angela, was nine years my senior. I was a product of her second and final marriage to Harry L. Drake. They named me Marion Elizabeth, but the family nicknamed me Papoose, a term for a Native American baby.

They gave me that nickname because they said I looked like an Indian baby when I was born, with a full head of shiny, dark hair. Eventually, they shortened Papoose to Poose, and that was what I was called within my immediate family and by my other relatives. My paternal grandmother, Dorothy, was the only one who insisted on calling me Marion.

My siblings and I called our parents by different names. They called my father by his given name, so I started doing the same. They called our mother either "Mama" or "Mother". I called her by her given name because I just felt more comfortable that way.

Reuben Jr., the oldest, lived in Chicago with his wife, daughters, Adrienne and Tiffany, and son, Dimitri. My mother's other children were in California.

I don't know if my parents chose California because of the weather or because most of their children lived there. Whatever the reason, I was glad I would be with Sharon's daughter, Sheri, again. I had grown used to playing with her when she and her mother lived with us in Chicago.

I had mixed feelings about leaving. I knew I would miss our spacious house, my pets, and some of the neighborhood kids. I would have said I'd miss my collie, Sunny, but my father left our gate open, and Sunny ran away. We never found him.

I would also miss Anton's daughter, Tammi, who lived on the next block. I really loved playing with Tammi. She was sweet, gentle, and easy to get along with.

Still, I was excited to reunite with Sheri. Although I found her aggravating at times, I had grown attached to her. We competed at everything. We used to race each other down the sidewalk on our block in Chicago. Being three years older, I always won, but before she left for California, she was catching up fast.

I didn't mind leaving Chicago too much because our home felt like a funeral parlor. My mother was devastated over losing both the restaurant and the house. She cried nearly every day, and when she wasn't crying, she was blaming my father for what she called his failures, which she said had caused our losses.

After enduring her sadness and blaming for a while, I was more than willing to leave. I hoped California would be a place where I could be happy again.

I smiled as my parents told me about the beaches, the sunny weather, and the amusement parks. It sounded like it was going to be a lot of fun. When it came time to pack my suitcases, I was ready to go.

I boarded the plane, and made the trip.

When I arrived in California, a family member picked me up and drove me to Don's apartment. Don was the second oldest after my brother Reuben. On the drive to Don's, I had a strange premonition that moving without my parents might be a mistake. I couldn't put my finger on it, but something didn't feel right.

When I arrived, I felt oddly uneasy. They seemed happy to see me, but I didn't feel particularly welcome.

At Don's apartment, I reacquainted myself with his wife, Audrey, and his stepkids, who were all around my age. I was surprised that Don had only a two-bedroom apartment with so many kids. He and Audrey slept in one bedroom, while their three children were crammed into the other.

I wasn't used to seeing people living like this. *They're packed in like sardines*, I thought.

Then there was the cigarette smoke.

As I walked through their front door, I stepped into a living room hazy with it. I looked around. People were smoking, and ashtrays and alcohol were on the coffee and end tables. *Whoa*, I thought. *What is this?*

My parents kept alcohol in the house, but it was never left out like this, and smoking inside was strictly forbidden. They knew it wasn't healthy. The cigarette smoke made me uncomfortable, and I had to keep stepping outside to get fresh air.

*Who were these people?* I thought. They weren't the same siblings I had known in Chicago.

*But did you really know them?* asked a small, quiet voice in my head.

I had to admit that I did not. Not really.

What neither I nor my parents knew at the time was that whatever their life had been before, it was gone. Their life now revolved almost entirely around drugs, sleazy characters, and alcohol.

California's promises of sunshine and happiness were as false as the smiles greeting me at Don's door.

# 2

# Charles' House

Soon after my arrival in California, I went to live with Sharon and her kids in her boyfriend Charles' home in Carson. Charles and Sharon occupied the master bedroom, Sheri and I shared a bedroom, and Sharon's son, Ricky, had a bedroom to himself.

I wasn't impressed when I met Charles. He never seemed to smile or talk much. He spent a lot of time out in the garage doing who knows what. At the dinner table, he was a cold, quiet presence.

I loved food and always had a big appetite, but in this house, I often left the table unsatisfied. I was afraid to ask for seconds because I didn't want to be a burden. I could feel Charles' cold, disapproving eyes on me as I ate. Intuitively, I knew Charles didn't really want me there—he tolerated me only because I was his girlfriend's sister.

I started junior high school that year while Sheri and Ricky went to elementary school. We needed new school clothes, especially me, since the clothes I had were from elementary school, and the junior high school kids dressed much more grown-up.

To my chagrin, there was very little money for clothes. We had to make do with a few new items here and there, usually bought at the start of the school year. Then, at Christmas, we'd get a few more new things to wear.

Along with the clothes we couldn't afford, we also couldn't afford family outings, or any other kind of entertainment that cost money. Sharon wouldn't take us to the movies, amusement parks, or even the beach. She would give us bus fare when she had it. If we wanted to go somewhere, we had to team up with Don and Audrey's kids and fend for ourselves.

It quickly became apparent that Sharon and the rest of my siblings in California were broke. Although I didn't know it yet, what little money they had—sometimes before even paying bills—was spent on drugs and alcohol, but mostly drugs.

* * *

Then there were problems with Sheri.

She simply was not the same child as she had been back in Chicago. This new version of her didn't want to share her things with me—even when it was necessary.

For example, Sheri and I had one five-drawer dresser in our bedroom that Sharon instructed us to share. There were two drawers for her, two for me, and we were supposed to share the fifth drawer and the socks it contained. We called it "*the sock drawer*".

When Sharon put her foot down and told Sheri she had to share her socks, she sulked and cried. And cried and sulked.

This was one issue where Sharon didn't give in to her. There simply wasn't enough money to buy me new socks. I guess it didn't occur to Sheri that while she lived with me, her grandparents, and her mother in Chicago, I let her play with all of my toys, coloring books, and other belongings.

She had access to my bed, my blankets, and my books. Back then, I had a lot more than she did because my parents had more money, and I shared those things with her.

As soon as one problem with Sheri died down, another one popped up.

She was very whiny when she didn't get her way. The next issue arose one night when I had what she called "*throw-up burps*" and she couldn't handle it. She went crying to her mother, complaining that my burps smelled like vomit and were making her sick.

5

I wasn't doing anything on purpose. My stomach was upset, and I couldn't stop burping. Sharon called me in the room, looked disgusted, and told me to stop.

I couldn't though.

I wondered if it had crossed Sheri's mind to get out of my face and stop talking to me. Apparently not.

* * *

*Then Charles just disappeared.*

He left the house and never came back.

It was such a relief! I didn't ask where he was, and Sharon didn't volunteer the information.

Then something unsettling started to happen: Sharon began receiving other men into the bedroom she shared with Charles.

Sheri and I may have been kids, but we weren't stupid. We knew what was going on—although Sheri's younger brother Ricky was probably too naive to understand.

The men kept coming. Before long, it felt like Sharon had a revolving door in her bedroom.

It was shameful and disgusting. I watched them arrive, and I watched them leave.

The smiles they wore when they emerged from her bedroom disturbed me. Some of them had a downright lecherous quality about them.

It seemed like Sharon had a preference when it came to the men she rendezvoused with in California: *scum.*

Almost all of them were indecent—scam artists, drug addicts, even killers.

I kept expecting Charles to return as the days went by, but he never did.

* * *

Then one day, the house was foreclosed on.

It turns out someone had stopped paying the mortgage. I have no idea if it was solely Charles' responsibility or if Sharon was supposed to chip in.

Whatever the case, we were forced to leave.

We packed up all our belongings and managed to get out before the Sheriff came to throw us out.

Don dutifully showed up and helped us load everything into his car. He drove home, dropped off our things, and then came back for us.

On the drive to Don's house, I wondered how long we would have to stay there before we had someplace to call home again.

I also wondered if my parents knew what was going on.

# 3

# Turkeys and Trauma

One day, Sharon took us to the house of one of her male "friends." She told us we were going to some kind of potluck or barbecue.

I didn't know who this person was, and I didn't care to know. I had no desire to meet or be around any of her friends or boyfriends.

The weather that day was typical Southern California—sunny and pleasant. When we arrived, a group of people had already gathered in the backyard. The space was fairly large, with a buffet of food laid out on a rectangular table under a shaded area.

I stood next to Sharon and Sheri, sighing, hoping we wouldn't be there too long.

As I looked around, I saw something unexpected.

Toward the back of the yard stood a group of turkeys.

I had never seen a live turkey before, and I thought they were beautiful—much taller than I had imagined. I should have felt delighted, but instead, I felt uneasy.

Why were these wild turkeys standing around in someone's backyard? And why were there so many? I didn't count them, but there had to be at least ten of the majestic birds wandering near the fence.

Then her friend came into view, leading a group of men toward the turkeys. They were loud, boisterous, and uncouth.

Suddenly, my blood ran ice cold as one of them grabbed a turkey and violently wrung its neck right there, in front of adults and children alike.

The men pounced on the remaining turkeys, grabbing them one by one and doing the same thing.

The backyard erupted into chaos.

The birds screamed, their headless bodies flailed wildly, flopping across the yard in spasms of death.

The sight was horrific.

I squeezed my eyes shut and clamped my hands over my ears.

*Please! Please! Please make it stop!* My mind screamed in terror.

Sharon seemed flustered and disturbed, but I wasn't sure why. Was she finally realizing how barbaric and traumatic this was? Or was she worried that I would tell our parents what I just had witnessed?

Either way, she sprang into action. Turning us away from the bloody spectacle, she rushed us inside through the patio door, shaking her head and muttering something about them killing the turkeys.

Even now, the sound of their screams haunts me.

The memory of their flopping, bloody, headless bodies—their lives violently snuffed out—is the stuff of nightmares.

But it wasn't just the turkeys that died that day. Something inside me shattered, too. A small, fragile trust that Sharon could, and would, protect us.

# 4

# Strung Out and Checked Out

When we arrived at Don's apartment in Long Beach after leaving Charles' house, I felt forlorn and dejected. Don and his wife Audrey's two-bedroom apartment was small. They slept in one bedroom, and Audrey's three children slept in the other. Feeling homeless and unwanted, I took my belongings into their kids' bedroom, along with Sheri and Ricky, and tried to make the best of it.

It was very crowded, both in the bedrooms and the rest of the apartment. All of us kids were fighting for space. The atmosphere was tense, and there were frequent arguments and fights among us.

It was here that Sharon's drug use became glaringly obvious, and it was here where she began to seriously neglect us.

There was a lot of cigarette smoke floating around in the air because all the adults—and most, if not all, of their friends—smoked. Don and Audrey had a lot of friends, so there were people around often. Occasionally, relatives would come over.

The kitchen had only one small refrigerator, which had to store perishable food for nine people. Audrey, and sometimes her daughters, cooked for their family, and Sharon cooked for me and her kids.

* * *

Before long, the partying started. They had house parties, and all the kids were relegated to the kids bedroom until it was over. While we waited, we tried to keep ourselves occupied with homework or other activities, keeping the window open for fresh air.

Then came the outside partying, where the women would go out on the town.

I would watch as Sharon put on her makeup. She would line her eyes with thick, black kohl eyeliner, slip into her party clothes, and head out the door. At first, she made sure we were fed and had what we needed for the night. But soon, she started leaving without feeding us.

All the kids in the apartment were left without adequate food. We would sit around in the living room, hungry, waiting for the adults to come back. Sometimes, we fought over the little food we were able to scrounge up.

Then Sharon started bringing the party inside.

I don't remember if it was in Don's apartment, or somewhere else, but one night, I was sitting in the living room, hungry, with a bunch of kids. We looked up as Sharon came in with several dubious-looking men and women trailing behind her. They made a beeline for the bedroom. One of them closed the door behind them.

We waited for Sharon to come out, to feed us, to take care of Ricky.

Finally, after awhile, they all emerged, glassy-eyed and kind of floating. Sharon, like the rest of them, was stoned.

There was no question in my mind by this time—Sharon was a full-on drug addict.

The others bumbled out the front door. Sharon turned her back on us, walked into the kitchen, and started putting together something for us to eat—never meeting our eyes, never offering any explanation or apology for her behavior or for making us wait to eat.

* * *

One time, Sharon took us to one of her friend's house. The house was full of people drinking and socializing.

11

I wandered through a wide walkway into one of the family rooms and came across a rambling, disheveled drunk. He looked straight at me and called me a motherfucker.

Shocked, blinking, and keeping an eye on him, I backed out of the room. When I got back to where Sharon and Sheri were standing, I was shaken. My instinct was to run up to Sharon and tell her what the man had called me—but I didn't.

Shaking my head, I tried to clear my thoughts. *Did I hear this man, right? Did he really call me that?* I wondered. *Was I scared to tell? If so, why?*

Thankfully, we eventually left the party and went home. I didn't tell Sharon or anyone else about my strange, upsetting encounter. I had no answers for the questions I asked myself, and I didn't know why. I pushed it out of my mind.

But that night, my anger and resentment simmered just below the surface.

\* \* \*

We continued to make do in Don's crowded apartment. Sheri and I were still attending school in Carson. Our cousins who lived in Carson let us use their address so we didn't have to switch schools. One of the adults in the house would pick us up after school and bring us back to Don's place. Don and Audrey's kids attended Long Beach schools.

Then came one terrible night.

I was sitting around with Sharon's kids and a few other nieces and nephews, waiting for her to come home and feed us. Of course, she left us to take care of Ricky. We kept taking turns looking out the front door, hoping to see her coming.

One of the kids peeked outside and spotted a cab pulling up to the courtyard entrance. She pulled her head back inside, turned to us, and whispered, "They're coming." I, along with several other kids, got up to look out the door.

What came next was horrendous.

Sharon and another woman came stumbling out of the cab, hanging on to each other to keep from falling. Unsteady on their feet, they rushed through the courtyard and into the apartment. One of the kids quickly closed the door behind them.

Their faces came into view in the living room light, and I cringed.

They were as high as a kites, pumped full of drugs.

All of a sudden, the woman with Sharon collapsed against the door. I watched in horror as her face contorted into something grotesque—it looked like The Tasmanian Devil on a rampage, tongue hanging out, eyes rolling in the sockets. Then, just as suddenly, her face snapped back to normal. She pushed herself off the door and resumed talking as if nothing had happened.

I had never seen anything like it.

Years later, I wondered if it had been a demonic manifestation meant to scare the children.

One of the kids burst into tears. I turned away in disgust. *What in the world had they taken? Is somebody going to die tonight?*

They had traumatized everyone in the apartment.

After the kids were calmed down, we were finally able to eat.

"Eat and go to bed!" Sharon snapped, avoiding our eyes, her expression a mix of guilt and defiance. She threw together a meal, shoving plates at us like we were a burden she couldn't wait to get rid of.

I was so thankful to be in bed, with the door closed, away from her. Again, I was determined to put the events of this terrible evening out of my mind—at least for now.

That night, in the darkened bedroom, my thoughts churned restlessly.

There was no question—evil was here. I could feel it. The fear, the uncertainty, the heaviness in the atmosphere. It was right here in the apartment with us, brought in by a few selfish junkies who cared more about their next fix than they did about the welfare of their own children.

This wasn't the example our parents had set. They didn't use drugs, and they didn't approve of them.

It was shameful how far into the gutter my siblings in California had fallen.

I didn't know what to do, where I could go, or how long I could put up with this.

*Was it time to call my parents and tell them what was going on?* I wondered. *Or should I just deal with it until they get here?*

I slipped into a troubled sleep without any answers.

# 5

# Wings Too Soon

We found out that Don's family was growing when Audrey announced she was pregnant one day. Besides Audrey's three kids that lived with them, Don had three kids by two other women—one he had married back in Chicago. All three of his other kids lived on the East coast. However, Don and Audrey didn't have any children together yet, so we were all looking forward to their new baby joining the family.

Everybody seemed happy about the pregnancy announcement, except maybe Sharon. I had started to notice that when good things happened to others in the family outside of herself and her kids, she became jealous and envious.

For instance, Audrey bought a stackable washer and dryer for her family. Sharon saw it, came home, and snapped, "She shouldn't have bought that."

That's all she said. She never explained why she felt that way. I could think of no other reason, besides envy, why she wouldn't want her own brother and his family to own a new appliance that would make their life easier.

Another time, Sharon called Audrey a "bitch" to her face. Later, in one of her uncontrollable rages, she hurled the same insult at me—this time in front of her son Asion. Then she stood back and watched as Asion disrespected me, doing nothing to stop him.

Our family happily awaited the birth of the new baby. When he finally arrived, he was beautiful and angelic. I thought he resembled my brother. They named him Don Angelo after his father. I really liked the name; I thought it was very creative.

They brought him home from the hospital and everything seemed to be going okay. Don and Audrey had set up his crib in the living room so Tracy and Terri, their two teenage daughters, could look after him when they were sleeping. Don and Audrey promptly went out and had the baby professionally photographed.

They had a metal frame made out of his baby shoes to frame the picture. It was proudly displayed in their home. Baby Don Angelo looked so innocent and sweet, though he also seemed a little fragile to me.

One terrible morning, Tracy got up and went over to Don Angelo's crib to check up on him. He wasn't breathing. She panicked and rushed in their room to wake up Don and Audrey. They frantically tried to revive him, but couldn't. Desperate, they called 911. The paramedics arrived, couldn't revive the baby either, and pronounced him dead.

Audrey, overcome with grief, ran out into the busy street in front of the apartment and right into oncoming traffic. In that moment, she didn't want to live anymore since Don Angelo couldn't.

It was a horrific loss. The funeral was very sad, with Don Angelo in his little white coffin and everybody crying and grieving.

After the funeral, we tried to recover and continue with life as usual. But we were heartbroken because little Don Angelo had grown his wings unexpectedly, and far too soon, and had flown up to Heaven, leaving us all behind to think of what could have been.

# 6

# Cedar Street

After we left Don's apartment, Sharon moved us into a roach-infested, two-bedroom apartment on Cedar Street. It was located in a poor, crime-ridden neighborhood.

Angela moved in soon after, bringing her young son, Eddie, as she had nowhere else to go. There was a lot of foot traffic in and out of the apartment—boyfriends, ex-boyfriends, drug dealers, friends, and acquaintances. They would sometimes sleep over, drink and smoke, and use the utilities. My brother Anton was over frequently as well. He was living with us part-time and somewhere else the rest of the time.

Most of the visitors were shady—both in character and appearance. You could sense it when they walked through the door. Sharon and Angela were drawn to people like this. In fact, they attracted parasitic relationships like a clothes dryer attracted lint.

Different parental figures floated around the apartment, trying to parent and offer advice to other people's children. None of it worked. These were people who couldn't even parent themselves or their own children, let alone anyone else's.

\* \* \*

More often than not, when their friends came over and started socializing, things became boisterous fairly quickly. It was as if they didn't know how to keep their voices down. The drinking and smoking were ever-present. I was allergic to cigarette smoke, but they didn't care. Their personal pleasure became before anyone or anything else. I had to leave the house frequently just to escape the smoke.

I never saw anything positive at the apartment. Positive interests and pursuits—like joining literary clubs, Bible studies, or taking trips to the library—seemed foreign to Sharon and Angela. Even sitting down with us kids and playing a simple board game like Monopoly never happened. Doing these things with us didn't interest them, and they didn't want to be bothered for our sake.

The Pacific Ocean and beach were about a twenty-minute drive from our dangerous, crime-ridden neighborhood, but Sharon and Angela never took us there. When we were old enough, we kids would band together with our cousins and go on our own.

We would scrape together loose change, gather towels, tote bags, make bologna sandwiches, and pack water and juice boxes—if we had them—before heading out on the bus to the beach. We usually made sure to be back before dark, hoping that we wouldn't come home to some horror scene waiting for us when we stepped over the threshold.

\* \* \*

Day to day life with Sharon and her family was completely miserable. I was very unhappy and depressed (though I didn't know it at the time) due to our living conditions, lack of entertainment funds, and Sharon's ever present preferential treatment of Sheri.

Sharon took everything Sheri said to heart, and everything I said with a grain of salt. She would always take Sheri's side and believe her version of the story whenever Sheri and I argued or had different accounts of an event.

She even made me wash the dishes when it was Sheri's turn once.

Whoever's turn it was to wash the dishes had to do them for the entire day. The next day, it would be the other person's turn. However, if someone didn't wash the night dishes on their assigned day, they would have to get up in the morning to do them.

One night, Sheri didn't wash her dishes when it was her turn. The next morning, she didn't want to do them either. We both ran to Sharon, expecting her to settle the dispute. She listened impatiently, then ignored our rule and made me wash them instead.

I did it, but I filed it away in my mind as just one more injustice—one more thing Sharon would eventually end up paying for.

I felt very sad and angry that she treated me, her own sister, this way. I felt like an orphan, someone she didn't want to be bothered with. I was certain that if she weren't so beholden to my parents, she wouldn't let me live with her.

I don't remember Sharon working until we moved to Cedar Street. Here, she started looking for a job and found one. Her work schedule varied—some days she worked late, coming home after dark. With Sharon working late several days a week, my brother Anton stepped in to parent us.

For a while, Anton tried to handle a sensitive situation with Sharon's son, Ricky, that she should have been handling herself. But, Anton got it terribly wrong.

One evening, I walked into the bedroom where the boys slept and saw Anton holding Ricky upside down by his ankles, whipping him with a belt. Ricky was screaming his head off.

Anton was convinced Ricky was acting out on purpose, but it was Sharon's job to parent her son. She let the abuse of her son continue, which deeply disturbed me.

There are still too many nights when these memories play their unwelcome imagery across my mind, shattering my sleep with terror and grief.

\* \* \*

Before long, the neighbors started noticing that the children in our apartment were being neglected. They began whispering and talking about Sharon behind her back. Some even gave her dirty looks when she stepped outside.

One day Lana—a lady Sharon befriended who lived down the street—came over for a visit. I was sitting in the living room with her and Sharon, eating a fried pork chop smothered in ketchup.

Lana took one look at my plate, frowned, and said, "Baby, you can't eat that. That pork chop ain't done."

"Oh, that's just ketchup," I said, realizing she mistook it for blood and thought the pork chop was raw.

Lana gave me a look that said *Are you sure?*, but reluctantly accepted my explanation and went back to talking with Sharon.

Lana had a violent tendency and a few loose screws.

One night, we saw her chasing a man down the street with a large butcher knife—barefoot. She looked like she had completely lost her mind.

After that, Sharon stopped fraternizing with her.

Even so, Lana's suspicions of neglect were shared by many of the other neighbors.

* * *

One day, Sharon was in her bedroom sleeping when her son, Ricky, was struck by a car.

Angela's son, Eddie, was also in the street when the car hit, but he managed to drop underneath the car to avoid being hit. The driver was speeding, and we could hear the screeching tires as they slammed on the breaks.

Someone woke Sharon up, and she stumbled out of bed, running outside to check on Ricky. By this time, a crowd had gathered. We assured her paramedics were on the way, and she ran back inside, returning with blankets for Ricky to lie on.

Angela wasn't around either—meaning no one had been supervising Eddie. This was unsurprising.

By the sheer grace of God, both Ricky and Eddie survived. Ricky suffered a broken clavicle, but thankfully, it healed after he came home from the hospital.

However, the incident only added to the growing whispers among the neighbors.

It was yet another sign, to them, that Sharon was a neglectful mother—and they didn't hesitate to talk about her behind her back.

\* \* \*

While all this was going on, I trudged through high school with low grades.

My grades had been sky-high almost all through elementary school, except for my last year in Chicago, when things started to go downhill. They didn't improve much while living with Sharon. Her cold, unfair ways—which I knew were mistreatment but didn't yet recognize as abuse—affected me more than I realized. I was unhappy and depressed, and it showed in my schoolwork.

I wasn't popular either. I was shy, quiet, and didn't have any real friends. I didn't have money to buy nice or stylish clothes. On top of that, I didn't think I was attractive.

I had a scar on my chin I got as a toddler after ripping it open on a chain-link fence due to my father's negligence. My parents said the doctors advised them to wait until I was older before attempting corrective surgery.

I was tired of waiting, but I also wondered where the money would come from when I was finally able to have the surgery.

Every time I caught a glimpse of the scar in the mirror, I saw a reminder of how little protection I'd had as a child—and how different I felt from everyone else.

And to put the sprinkles on the devil's cake, the elementary school kids used to tease me relentlessly about my scar, leaving me feeling even more isolated and bullied.

I never told my parents. I think it was because I was so ashamed of being teased.

# 7

# Hollywood Dreams

I hadn't been living with Sharon long before I became aware that she, along with a few in-laws and baby mamas, had dreams of making it big in Hollywood. They wanted to sing, dance, model, and act. They wanted to form bands, be signed by mega music companies, and obtain lucrative modeling contracts.

The only problem with that was they had no talent. I can say without a doubt that I saw nothing from them that even came close to approaching the talent needed in order to achieve such stardom.

I never saw or heard about them working toward those goals by doing things like taking singing or acting lessons. So, I chalked it up to a pipe dream and didn't think I would see any of these lofty dreams come to fruition—until one day I witnessed what they thought was their breakthrough moment.

But there was nothing lofty about it.

Sharon had a group of women over one day for socializing. They brought their kids. I was there, along with Sharon's kids and Don and Audrey's girls. The kids ran in and out while the adults mingled in the living room, the kitchen, and out on the front porch. As usual, the cigarettes and alcohol flowed freely.

It was Southern California, and they dressed accordingly—but their clothes were skimpy, and they seemed to be getting skimpier and skimpier with each gathering.

Halter tops without bras, shorts worn super short and wedged up in their crotches, the bottom portion of their buttocks bulging out beneath the fabric. They wore sandals and flip-flops on their polished toenails painted pink and various shades of red.

*Red is for harlot*, I thought.

I looked at the women with distaste. I was relieved my cousin Justine wasn't involved in this group of clueless individuals and their misguided aspirations of stardom.

Justine, my first cousin on my father's side, lived in a city adjacent to ours. She had three children: two adorable little girls, Erika and Arnetha, and a cute little boy named Arkel. Sometimes, we would babysit them while she worked.

Justine had very colorful nicknames for the girls. Erika was nicknamed *Stinky* and Arnetha was nicknamed *Dookey*. I believe the nicknames alluded to the messes they made in their diapers as babies and toddlers.

I thought it was hilarious.

When the girls became old enough to go to school, Justine asked us not to use their nicknames anymore out of fear they would be teased by other children. We respected her wishes and henceforth started calling them by their given names.

I was sitting on the carpet among the other kids, trying to catch the adults' latest juicy gossip while pretending I was focused on something else—as young girls tend to do. My parents were fond of saying, "Little pitchers have big ears."

Yes, we did—and we heard plenty.

As the women laughed and sipped their drinks, one of the kids, who was a couple years older than me, handed me a photo album.

"Take a look," she said, her voice dripping with mischief.

I opened the album and gasped.

I remember it as if it were happening in slow motion.

It was a photograph of Sharon. She was naked and arranged in the most lewd, distasteful pose I had ever seen. She had this goofy, come-hither grin on her face.

I could see she was trying to look sexy—but instead she looked silly.

Her dark brown hair hung long and straight down around her shoulders.

She was sitting on the photographer's floor, wearing a thick, long rope of beads around her neck, which was supposed to be artfully arranged around her breasts—*and nothing else.*

As my eyes traveled downward, I could see that her legs were wide open, and the picture faded and darkened mercifully so the viewer could both see—and not see—the dark cavern of lust between her legs.

I cringed.

I tore my eyes away and turned the page.

On the next page, a family baby mama was naked and running across a field of grass. She had some kind of adornment around her neck, too.

I had to hurry up.

The grownups were coming back to where we were sitting. I closed the photo album and gave it back to my niece, who put it back in the place where she had found it.

I was floored.

I didn't have any words.

*This was it?* I thought. *This was how they were going to become models? Degrading themselves in sleazy photos?*

Later on, I wondered if they thought these pictures were going to land them in *Playboy* magazine then shoot them into the stratosphere of stardom as Playboy Bunnies. These photos weren't dignified enough for Playboy—maybe Hustler.

No, no. These pictures weren't a ticket to stardom.

They were a window into the desperation of women chasing dreams they were never equipped to achieve.

# 8

# Cuckoo for Carnage

I woke up thirsty one night and slowly made my way toward the door in our darkened bedroom, heading to the kitchen.

Grasping the doorknob, I pushed, then paused, as I heard voices thick with emotion coming from the living room. It sounded like Anton, Angela, and Sharon.

I kept the door cracked as I stood there, looking on as I listened to their conversation. The three of them were sitting on the couch, in the midst of a fiery discussion.

Sharon was quickly looking from one of them to the other, her face twisted into an ugly mask of rage.

Suddenly, she spat out, "I want you both to help me beat his ass!"

Her voice was steadily rising in volume. I didn't know who she was talking about, but I gathered it was someone she was dating.

Then it was Anton's turn to speak, "Sharon," he said, his eyes pleading with her to calm down. He held up his hand, palm side outward, as if preparing to fend off a blow. "We can't just go over there and beat up this man for no reason!"

He looked over at Angela, who was sitting there silently, as if to say, *Jump in. Help me. Don't make me do all of the talking.*

Angela hesitated a moment, then looked at her and said cautiously, "Sharon, we can't—"

Suddenly, Sharon jumped up as if she had been shot out of a cannon. A look of complete lunacy came over her face. It looked like a combination of rage and a mental breakdown. Eyes wild and staring up at the ceiling, arms flailing wildly about her head—

"Aaghh, aaghh!" she cried out violently, her voice becoming deep and guttural.

She grabbed her car keys and ran outside, slamming the door behind her.

Angela and Anton looked at each other, bewildered and shell-shocked, as if to say, *What the fuck was that?* They looked like they had just seen a tornado blow through the room.

At that moment, it seemed like they had connected the dots and realized there was something very wrong with Sharon—but I think they knew before that. And I think our brother Reuben Jr., the therapist, knew before any of us.

By this point, hearing the noise, the other kids started stirring in their beds, beginning to wake up. Not really knowing what to think—because the chaos was a regular part of my life now—I quietly closed the door and crept back to bed.

As I struggled to get back to sleep, I wondered what had caused her to become the narcissistic monster she was. Cruel, heartless, and vengeful. As the months and years dragged by, I could no longer deny what she was.

She was like a malevolent spider, spinning a web and lying in wait to trap the unsuspecting and suck them dry.

As I tried to understand her over the years, and thankfully not very often, my mind went back to what I witnessed one day while I was in the apartment in Chicago she shared with Ricky's father, Ricardo.

That was a day I wanted to forget—but couldn't.

Sharon instigated a fight with Ricardo right before they were due to move their family to California. They weren't married, but they were a couple with a new baby.

Sharon and Ricardo were in the hallway when it started. Sheri and I watched as Sharon kept taunting him while he stayed silent. She kept egging him on, inviting him to come into the bedroom with her and fight, while it looked like he was trying to get away from her.

"C'mon! C'mon!" She sneered, baring her teeth, getting up in his face and circling him.

I was just a little kid, but even I knew this wasn't going to end well.

As the argument progressed, I could sense the heightened anxiety and fear coming off of Sheri, who was standing beside me.

Finally, he went into the bedroom with her and shut the door.

After a few moments, we heard multiple sounds of a body being slammed into the wall. *Thump. Thump. Thump.* The thumps were loud and continuous, and the bedroom walls shook with each heavy impact. Sheri was already crying by this point.

Suddenly, the door was flung open, and Ricardo walked out, dragging Sharon behind him by her hair. She looked like she had been run over by a truck.

Her long brunette hair was disheveled and all over her head, so we couldn't see her face. She wasn't saying anything because Ricardo had beaten the breath out of her.

Ricardo stood there with a fistful of her hair firmly in his grasp. As Sheri broke out into piercing screams, Ricardo dragged Sharon into the middle of the floor and dumped her there like a bag of garbage.

I felt numb as I stared into the hallway.

I was sorry my big sister was hurt, but I didn't know what to think. I really didn't.

I had never seen a woman beaten like that. I had never seen *anyone* beaten like that.

My parents had arguments that sometimes became volatile, but Harry never beat Mag. In fact, Mag was often the aggressor in their relationship. This was inconceivable to me.

Eventually, I was taken back home to my parents. I never told them what happened.

I have no idea why.

Maybe I thought Sharon was going to tell them. I didn't know.

After the beating, Sharon stayed with Ricardo.

Months later, they packed up and moved to California, taking Sheri and Ricky with them.

Less than two years later, Ricardo had bailed from her life.

Hearing the other kids talking quietly in their beds, I forced my mind back into the present.

Weary, and trying to put the night's chaos behind me, after awhile, I fell back asleep.

# 9

# Infected and Neglected

We found out that Angela had been letting one of her homeless lovers sleep in our beds while we were at school. He had been at the apartment several times. He looked like somebody she had dragged out of the garbage bin out back.

Angela had been troubled for a long time. When she was a child living in Chicago, she ran away from home several times. She had a hair-trigger temper and was prone to violence. Like Sharon, she had never successfully made any of her relationships with men stick, and she kept getting involved with *Mr. Wrong* time and time again. This time was no different.

One day, I came home from school to find her lover snuggled up and sleeping in one of our beds. Sheri had discovered him as well, and we immediately told Sharon. This man was filthy and unkempt, and after he slept on our sheets, they were discolored with dirt and reeked of his putrid body odor. They had started out white but ended up beige.

Sharon told Angela he couldn't sleep there anymore, and thankfully, we didn't find him in our beds again. It was definitely a lot easier to breathe once he was gone.

Hygiene in the apartment was a constant issue. People shared personal items like combs and hairbrushes, and the apartment itself wasn't regularly cleaned. Sharon and Angela never taught me anything—how to cook, clean a house, or sew. I had to figure everything out for myself later in life when I moved into my own home.

We didn't have a washer or dryer in the apartment, so we had to take our clothes to the laundromat. Sometimes I went with Sharon to help, and other times, I went with a guy from the next block who I had befriended and eventually started dating. We would go to the laundromat together and wash our clothes at the same time.

One day, I noticed a sore, swollen area on the top of my head. It was red, tender, and painful to the touch. Gingerly, I parted my thick, long hair and looked at it in the mirror. It was hard to see through all my hair, but I could feel a rounded bump. Parts of it were flaky and crusty. I showed it to Sharon, who examined it but couldn't figure out what it was. Resigned, she finally took me to the doctor.

I don't remember the exact diagnosis, but I believe the doctor told Sharon it was caused by coming into contact with germs from dirty linens or clothing. I was completely grossed out. My mind went back to that filthy man in our beds, possibly using our towels and washcloths, and even our combs and brushes.

I felt like a dirty little animal out in the wild—a diseased rodent that had picked up something disgusting while rummaging through a dumpster for its next meal.

The doctor carefully shaved and clipped the hair growing through and around the lesion, which had now reached a diameter about the size of a golf ball.

He applied medicated ointment, wrote Sharon a prescription for a medicated cream, and gave us instructions on how to apply it at home. It eventually healed, but I suffered permanent hair loss in that area of my scalp.

After my scalp healed, my brother Don's daughter Tracy, who was skilled at braiding hair, offered to braid mine. I let her, and she did a great job, but unfortunately, the way she arranged the braids emphasized the area where the lesion had been. Sharon took one look at my hair and scoffed, "I don't like it."

Before that doctor's visit, I couldn't even remember the last time I had seen a doctor in California. Medical visits were rare in Sharon's house—so were dentist visits. She only took us to the dentist when it was absolutely necessary.

One day, she had no choice. We needed cleanings and some minor dental work, so she took us to the dentist's office. When it was my turn, I sat down nervously in the treatment chair, my hands clenched together.

The dentist reclined my chair and examined my teeth, poking around with his dental tools. After a few minutes, he straightened up and exclaimed in frustration, "This girl has a quarter-inch of tartar on her teeth! This is ridiculous!"

He turned to his dental assistant, shaking his head.

I was extremely embarrassed and wanted to shrink down in the chair and disappear. The dentist grumbled the entire time he cleaned my teeth.

When I got back to the apartment and told Sharon what he had said, she dismissed it with an eye roll. "He needs to do his job and stop complaining," she remarked.

I had to endure several more visits before all the tartar was finally scraped off my teeth.

Around this time, Angela had started consulting Sharon about her gynecological health. Her drug use had clouded her judgment, making her behavior erratic and inappropriate. One day, in an attempt to explain something, Angela hiked up her skirt and exposed herself—right in an area of the apartment where children could see.

I was in the room when it happened, and I wished I were anywhere else. Disgusted, I turned away as swiftly as I could, but not before witnessing something I never should have seen. Granted, we were sisters, but I was still a minor, and her behavior was extremely inappropriate.

That image stayed with me far longer than it should have. It wasn't just what I saw—it was the unsettling realization that, in this household, boundaries meant nothing. In fact, there were no boundaries.

What should have been a moment of embarrassment or regret for Angela was treated as just another inappropriate act in a place where decency had long since eroded.

I left the room that day, but the feeling of violation lingered—another stain on an already broken home.

# 10

# Ambushed by Thugs

I t was difficult making friends on Cedar Street because many of the adults and kids were criminals. It was a rough group. Some of the kids had access to knives and guns. Sheri made friends easily, but she didn't seem to care about their character. She could make friends with anybody. I was the opposite—if someone wasn't inherently good, I saw no value in a friendship with that person.

It dawned on me Sheri was learning from her mother. She had watched the kind of friends and men her mother chose, and she was choosing the same kind of people to associate with.

Many times, Sheri stayed with her friends while I hung around in front of the apartment, hoping I would meet someone I wanted to socialize with. Against my better judgment, I started talking to a couple of girls my age, June and Leona. They lived across the street in a rented house. Sometimes, I'd go and hang around their front yard, and sometimes they came to mine. They had a two story-house, and it was overflowing with people.

One day, I walked outside, and one of them called me over. As I walked up the driveway, I stopped in my tracks. I looked around and up toward the balcony of the house. There were a lot of people standing around. They had a big family, and I thought some of them must be their cousins.

They looked mean, like they were ready to start something.

Suddenly, both June and Leona hit me. It must have been somewhere on my face or head, but I didn't feel it. What I *did* feel was intense anger that was about to turn into rage. I looked at all the backup they had, all the support, and I didn't want to fight in their driveway. There were too many of them, and I didn't know what they were going to do.

So, I turned around, crossed the street, and went back into my apartment.

I was too ashamed to tell anyone what had happened. Most kids would have told their family and figured out how to deal with it together. But I didn't see the point in telling mine. I had never gotten any support from them before.

*Why would it be different now?*

*All they're going to do is shame and abandon me,* I thought.

The word about what happened got around our block, and Sheri found out. She might have even looked out the window and saw it happening.

Then Sharon found out, and her solution was to bring my niece Terri over so I wouldn't have to fight two girls by myself.

Terri was about a year older than me. I didn't know if Sharon wanted us to start a fight, or wait for them to start something. She didn't tell me.

Terri and I went outside and hung around the front porch. It was turning dark out.

Suddenly, a large gangster-style sedan pulled up and stopped in the middle of the street in front of our apartment. The door opened, and Leona got out, posturing while staying close to the car. Then one of her older brothers got out, stood up threateningly, and then sat back down in the driver's seat.

They wanted us to come out in the street to fight her.

After a few minutes, Terri turned around and went into the house, and I followed her.

Sharon came into living room, took one look at us, and came unglued.

"Get your asses back outside!" she screamed wildly.

We did, but they were gone.

I was angry over the attack and thought Sharon and Sheri considered me a coward.

For months, I walked through the apartment complex that we used as a walkway, hoping I would find Leona and June alone so I could fight them.

A little over a year later, I was close to catching one of them alone when

Sheri and I were walking through the apartment walkway. It was Leona, but she was carrying her three-month-old son in her arms, which ruled out a confrontation.

Then something strange happened—Sheri started talking and laughing with June as if everything was normal, as if nothing had happened, as if June and Leona hadn't jumped me.

She even held and admired her baby.

*Unbelievable.*

I was angry, and I sulked as we walked away.

I didn't confront Sheri and ask why she had been friendly to someone who had jumped me because I knew she wouldn't give me a straight answer. She had learned how to gaslight from her mother.

And I didn't address it with Sharon because I knew she would take her daughter's side.

# 11

# Bonds and Betrayals

It was a nice sunny day, so Sheri and I decided to ride the bus to the mall. I was wearing sweats, and she had on shorts and a T-shirt; we both liked to dress casually.

We arrived at the mall, did some window shopping, then got into an argument. She threw my comb on the department store floor. I had no idea why she did it. Furious and embarrassed, I called her a "bitch." We went home and, as usual, Sheri portrayed me as the villain. And, as usual, Sharon took her side.

Anton came home later that night and believed Sheri until he heard my side of the story and understood why I did what I did. Then, he agreed that Sheri started the confrontation.

I lay in bed that night and replayed the day's events in my mind. Before I closed my eyes and tried to sleep, I contemplated my relationship with Sheri. I wasn't into astrology and reading horoscopes. However, I knew we were both born under the Aries zodiac sign, and we both had the typical Aries personality—competitive, determined, and stubborn.

As a result, we were always butting heads. In fact, most times we got along like oil and water.

*Would it always be this way?* I wondered as I slipped into a restless sleep.

I didn't want to fight with her—I wanted to be her friend. After all, we were growing up together like sisters.

I loved Sheri, and I knew she loved me because many years later, she sent me a letter telling me so. That letter made me extremely happy. She expressed her disappointment years later because I didn't write back, but I didn't know she was expecting a response. Besides, I wasn't comfortable or used to sharing emotions within the family because of the soul-destroying ways I had been treated.

In one of Sharon's more tender moments—few and far between when it came to me—she told me how when she was pregnant with Sheri, she *knew* she was having a girl because I always wanted to be up under her. It was like I knew my little friend was in that big belly, and I couldn't wait for her to come out and play with me.

Sheri and I had our differences, but deep down, I always believed we had an unbreakable bond.

She was the sister I never had.

I never imagined that one day, that bond would shatter in the worst possible way.

* * *

Sheri and I went to the mall another day and stumbled upon the John Robert Powers Modeling Agency. They had a storefront inside the mall. I wanted to go inside and see what it was about, so we opened the glass doors and ventured inside.

Everyone—both the students and the employees—looked fantastic. They were well-dressed, with expertly styled hair, skillfully applied makeup, and perfectly manicured nails.

In contrast, Sheri and I both had on a T-shirt and jeans, and I had my hair tied back in a messy ponytail.

Sheri was embarrassed because of how we were dressed, but I didn't care that much. I was too interested in learning how to become one of the elegant, fashionably dressed young women in the agency.

I thought if I could accomplish that, I could gain the self-esteem I needed to strike out on my own and have a happy, successful life one day.

A representative in a pristine gray skirt suit and heels led us into a luxurious conference room, complete with a large vase of fresh flowers on the long glass table.

We sat down as she gave us both brochures. I looked around the room and smiled, inhaling the fragrance of peonies and hydrangeas in various shades of pink and white permeating the air.

I listened excitedly as the representative described the program but was disappointed when I saw the price sheet. Nevertheless, I concentrated on the sales pitch.

After that part was over, the sales agent ushered us into the photography room, where they took a "before" picture of us in anticipation of enrolling in the program.

She explained that when we graduated from the program, they would take the "after" picture and compare the two.

"You two will be absolutely amazed at the change," she gushed enthusiastically in her little-girl voice. She told us the pictures would also be shown to prospective students with our permission.

She handed us her business card, told us to call her when we were ready to start the program, and walked us out.

On the ride home, I stared out the window, thinking about the John Robert Powers school and how I could come up with the money.

*I'd probably need to get a job*, I thought. That was probably going to be two or three years away, but I was willing to wait if I had to.

The school was both a modeling agency and a finishing school, and that excited me.

*I would love to try my hand at modeling*, I thought. *Or at least learn to walk, talk, and act like a model.*

\* \* \*

I put the John Robert Powers Modeling Agency out of my mind—at least until I could find a way to afford it—and focused on other things. Still, I often found myself dreaming about the school and everything related to modeling.

While I dreamed of attending the modeling school one day, an opportunity to be part of a fashion show arrived much sooner.

One day, Fatima, a friend of Sharon, Don, and Audrey, decided to put on a fashion show. She was supplying all the clothing, shoes, and makeup.

Fatima and her family were Muslim. I remember going over to their house with Sharon and Sheri one day and being impressed because they had one whole bedroom dedicated to prayer. It was appropriately dubbed "the prayer room."

Fatima invited Sheri and Terri to model in the show, but to my bitter disappointment, she didn't invite me.

When I asked Sharon about it, she offered a few feeble excuses but acted like she really didn't know why I wasn't invited.

I wanted Sharon to ask Fatima if I could participate. Instead, she kept gaslighting and brushing me off until it was time for the fashion show.

I went and forced myself to maintain an affable attitude throughout.

Sheri and Terri did a good job modeling. They looked really pretty with their makeup done, their hair skillfully styled, and the high-fashion clothing they were wearing.

It was one of the rare times I had ever seen Sheri wear makeup. She didn't believe in wearing it unless she felt the occasion absolutely warranted it.

I suspected that her prim, *Little House on the Prairie*-like attitude toward wearing makeup was a rejection of her mother's wantonness. She saw where it had gotten Sharon, and she did *not* want to go down that road.

I kept a civil attitude and congratulated them, but I wasn't happy. I felt that Sharon should have told Fatima that if I couldn't participate, Sheri wouldn't either.

Of course, she wasn't going to do that though.

On the ride home, it was all I could think about. I kept wondering why I was overlooked.

And, more importantly, why no one really cared.

* * *

On weekends and during the Summer when school was out, Mag and Harry, who had relocated to California by this time and landed on Sharon's couch, would take us with them to visit Mag's sister Tommie.

Aunt Tommie was Mag's older sister. My maternal grandmother, Lizzie, had given birth to four girls, two of whom were twins. Aunt Tommie lived in Los Angeles with her husband, Leo, and their children. They had a big family—around ten to twelve children.

I really liked this because I had always dreamed of being a part of a large family. Since most of Mag's other children were out of the house when I was growing up in Chicago and so much older than I was, I felt like an only child. At times, I remember being very lonely, growing up in that big house with no other children around.

For a few years, I had Sheri to play with. When she moved with her mother to California, Mag and Harry arranged for Donny and Kim, Don's two kids by his first wife, to come over and play with me. Those were fun and happy times while they lasted.

One day, Mag and Harry fell out with their mother, Winnie, and I was told Winnie wouldn't allow them to come over anymore. I was heartbroken. It would be more than twenty years before I saw them again.

Sure, I still had my niece, Tammi, who lived right down the street, to play with. But, Donnie and Kim were closer to my age. Sheri was three years younger than me, and Tammi was younger than her.

So, going over Aunt Tommie's and Uncle Leo's house with my parents and Sheri became something I looked forward to. With so many kids, their home was always bustling with people, and there was always something fun and interesting going on.

Uncle Leo and Aunt Tommie were always pleasant and welcoming. They were very easygoing people. My mother was very close to Aunt Tommie; they got along very well, and they resembled each other. Looking at them, it was easy to tell they were sisters. They had the same button nose they inherited from their father Arthur.

Uncle Leo was such a character. He pronounced Aunt Tommie's name with a long o vowel sound as in "Tony."

Many times, our cousin Raymond would visit, and we always had fun with him. We would sit at Aunt Tommie's breakfast table, talking and playing around.

We usually had some pocket change. If not, Raymond would ask Aunt Tommie, and Sheri and I would ask Harry for some money to go to the store. They'd usually give it to us, and then the three of us would walk to the store, talking and laughing, and bring back things like soda, candy, or chips.

On warmer days, we'd get ice pops—I loved the ones striped red, white, and blue, and shaped like a space rocket.

I loved the way Aunt Tommie's family interacted with each other. They were close knit and they supported each other. They also took care of their mother. I often saw one of my cousins—Betty, Cookie, or another—brushing or rolling up her hair.

They lived on one side of a duplex, with Betty and her kids, Latessa and Michael, on the other. During our visits, relatives and kids were always around, and I loved it because it was a happy environment.

Once, during a visit, they threw a "Heaven and Hell" party—I thought it was the epitome of creativity. The Heaven party took place on the ground floor, and the Hell party took place downstairs in the basement.

Most homes in Southern California didn't have a basement, so that was a happy and convenient bonus, and they put it to good use.

At the Heaven party, everyone was supposed to behave, and they served cake and non-alcoholic drinks like punch. At the Hell party, you could behave like you wanted, and wear what you wanted—within reason.

Down there, the music was cranked up, and the adults were allowed to smoke cigarettes or cigars and drink alcoholic beverages. The kids weren't allowed alcohol, of course, but I imagined one or more of my cousins probably spiked a bowl of punch down there somewhere as a prank.

Both children and adults circulated freely up and down the stairs that night, and it was a lot of fun. I stayed upstairs because I was kind of wary of the Hell party. Part of me was always shy, and I knew there were probably some friends of my cousins down there that I didn't know. Plus, the name "Hell" gave me considerable pause.

At that point, I had seen enough devil and demon movies, which were very scary, that I didn't like the word *Hell*. Even so, I was curious, so I was tempted to go downstairs and see what was happening.

But, I didn't; I stayed upstairs and enjoyed my cake and punch like a good little girl.

\* \* \*

One evening at our apartment on Cedar Street, Sheri and I were outside socializing with a few other kids. A couple of older guys, who we had seen cruising around the neighborhood a few times, drove up in their car and started talking to us. They looked to be in their late twenties or early thirties.

They were cheerful and engaging, and Sheri and I talked and laughed with them. They asked if they could take us for a ride in their car, and we said yes and got in. We were two giggly teenagers who found these two older guys intriguing, and basically, we didn't know any better. Sharon hadn't really taught us much, and she certainly never lead by example.

They drove us around the neighborhood. We didn't go far from home. They talked and tried to impress us with their knowledge and accomplishments while we listened and giggled. The pleasant fragrance of their crisp, woodsy aftershave filled the car.

After a while, they drove us home and dropped us off in front of our apartment. I had the feeling they would be back—that this car ride was just their way of getting to know us.

When we came back, it was dark outside, and Mag approached us and wanted to know where we had been. She followed us as we went into Sharon's room and took off our jackets.

We told her, and she became startled, flustered, and frantic. Gathering herself, she launched into an evangelistic, puritanical diatribe about the dangers of older men and getting into cars with strangers.

I noticed she was wearing one of her high-necked, prudish, long-sleeved cotton gowns that covered her almost from head to toe.

Besides warning us not to get into cars with strangers, she hammered it home again and again—*men only want one thing from women."*

After Mag finished, we nodded, promising not to do it again. She spun on her bare heel and abruptly left the room.

Later, she informed Sharon when she got home, and Sharon had a private conversation with Sheri about it. That was the end of it.

When we saw the two guys driving around in their car, we stayed away from them.

Mag was right, of course. Those guys could have raped or murdered us. Mag made her point, but it was the way she delivered the message and the outlandish things she said about men in general that gave me pause.

The way she talked and acted during that episode, and the ugly things she said about men, made me wonder if she had any skeletons in her closet.

*Had some bad man done something to her in her past that she couldn't bring herself to talk about?*

*If so, would I ever find out what had happened?*

# 12

## A Gnome's Fury

One day, I was in the living room when I heard raised voices coming from the apartment's only bathroom. I got up off the couch and walked into the small hallway to see what was going on. The bathroom door was slightly ajar, and when I peeked inside, I could see Angela arguing with Charles.

He had come back from wherever it was he had disappeared to back in Carson, and he and Sharon had resumed an unhealthy on-again, off-again relationship. He was the same old Charles—mean, abusive and extremely unattractive. He reminded me of a short, ugly, disgruntled gnome from some dark, twisted fairy tale gone wrong. Whenever he visited Sharon, he invariably greeted everybody with a frown.

He wasn't happy with all the people Sharon currently had living in her house and didn't hesitate to tell her so.

"You got your mama over there laying on your couch..." Mag overheard him growl one day to Sharon in her bedroom.

After hearing that, Mag turned around and went back into the living room and was upset for the rest of the day.

The voices from the bathroom, laced with profanity, were growing louder. Angela had been straightening her hair when the argument began; I could see the hot comb in its cradle sitting on the counter. Traces of steam still lingered in the air, as if someone had recently taken a shower.

Suddenly, Charles' face twisted into an ugly mask of fury. He picked up the straightening comb, clasped it in his right fist, and struck Angela in the jaw. Her head snapped back as surprise and pain registered in her eyes.

My eyes now as big as saucers, I put my hand over my mouth to quiet a small gasp that escaped. I backed away from the crack in the door so they wouldn't see me.

I listened as Charles resumed ranting and raving at Angela in the small, cramped bathroom. He threatened more violence as he held the straightening comb high over her head in his fist. He glared at her, and the message in his menacing stare couldn't have been clearer—Open your mouth again, and I'll close it for you.

I backed away slowly and went back to sit on the couch. I knew I would have to call someone if Charles became violent again. I grabbed a magazine off the coffee table and pretended to read. A few minutes later, he stormed out.

A little while later, Mag, Harry, and Don returned from the store, their arms full of grocery bags.

Angela was still in the bathroom working on her hair when our parents and brother walked through the door. Still shaken, she came out and began telling them what had happened. Her voice, heightened with emotion, rose and fell as she recounted the attack.

She ended her story by saying, "He didn't have to hit me," breathing hard between the words.

Don stuck around awhile, perhaps to confront Charles when he returned or at least to get his side of the story. Charles didn't come back that day though, and eventually Don went home to his family.

Sharon came home from work and talked to Angela in private.

I wasn't aware of any repercussions for Charles following their conversation. Nor was I expecting any.

# 13

# Blood Sister

Angela continued her drug use and she was now high more often than she was sober. She was also constantly angry.

Then one day, she turned her anger on me.

I was in the living room and had just woken up from a nap when an argument started between us.

I was lying on the couch when she came over and straddled me. The next thing I knew, she had slipped her hands around my throat and began to strangle me. I reached up and struggled to pry her hands from my throat. She didn't let go. Instead she began to squeeze harder and harder as I struggled to breath.

I looked up into her soulless, bloodshot eyes as I started to panic. They gleamed with a murderous intent. At this point, I was gasping for air as I fought to get her hands off my neck.

Sharon, who had been asleep in her room, heard the commotion and rushed into the living room. She saw what was happening and hurried to separate us. She maneuvered herself between us and helped pry Angela's fingers off my neck.

When we were finally separated, disoriented and trying to breath normally again, I lunged at Angela with blind rage.

Angela, a much better street fighter, anticipated my move. She rushed in to close the space between us and punched me in the face. Hard.

Sharon stood there a moment surveying the situation. Then, as if weighing whether to intervene again, she turned and walked back to her room—just like she often did when things became too chaotic.

I whirled around, ran to the phone, and called my aunt Tommie, who lived in Los Angeles. Mag and Harry, who were visiting her, had left her phone number in case of an emergency.

Aunt Tommie answered after a couple of rings. I asked for my parents and blurted out what Angela had done to me. They had gone to the store, but Aunt Tommy promised to tell them as soon as they got back. I could hear the concern in her voice.

I went back to the couch and lay down, hoping my parents would either call or come home soon.

They returned not long after, checked to make sure I was okay, and had a talk with Angela. They were fed up and angry. I didn't hear what was said, but I hoped there would be no more assaults from her in my future.

Turns out, I hoped in vain.

* * *

A few months later Angela put her hands on me again.

We got into an argument outside of one of the bedrooms. I don't even recall what it was about. Angela was high on drugs again—and becoming aggressive. Her glassy eyes were filled with anger. I decided to stop talking and just walk away.

Just then Angela picked up a knife from somewhere, grabbed my wrist, and cut.

My skin sliced open like butter.

The cut was about an inch and a quarter long. It was deep, too—so deep that the fat layer was visible beneath the blood.

Thinking she had cut a major blood vessel and that I was going to die, I started crying, trembling, and clutching my wrist as I backed away from Angela.

I couldn't believe it. *Did this bitch really just cut me?* I asked myself.

Sheri had been watching from the shadows. She walked past us, into the living room, and out the front door. Later, someone told me she had been outside talking and socializing like nothing had happened.

I stood there, cradling my bleeding wrist, and it seemed like only moments later that Mag, Harry, and Don entered the apartment. They saw me crying and clutching my wrist and rushed over. When they got close enough to see the wound, Mag burst into tears while Harry stormed angrily from the room.

She turned to Don and sobbed. "I'm scared of what Harry might do," she said in hushed tones, crying on his chest.

Then, something upsetting and frightening happened—Don sprang into action.

He grabbed Angela and began to beat her with his fists—and he was *very* handy with his fists.

I couldn't see into the living room from where I was standing, but I heard Angela's screams and the sounds of his fists connecting with her body.

Someone wrapped a blanket around my shoulders and hustled me out the front door. We were on our way to the emergency room. I don't remember seeing Angela as I left the apartment.

Once outside, we started walking across the street toward Mag and Harry's car. Just as we reached it and were about to get in, several police cars pulled up in the street next to us and in front of the apartment.

Moments later, Angela stumbled out onto the porch.

My eyes widened. She looked like she had just gone twelve rounds with Mike Tyson.

I had no idea she had been beaten that badly. Her face was swollen and unrecognizable, one eye was blackened, and her body looked battered. Tears streamed down her face as she cried uncontrollably.

She pointed Don out to the police, and they approached him cautiously. But after Don pointed to my wrist and explained that Angela cut me, the police started getting back into their cars to leave.

Angela, still crying and trembling on the porch, called out to them desperately.

"Wait! Wait! Are y'all just going to leave? Aren't you going to arrest him?

Look at the way he beat me!" she screamed.

One of the cops, who had opened his car door and was about to get in, looked up and called out to her in a booming voice, "No! You cut your sister!"

With that, they got into their vehicles and got the hell out of Dodge.

Harry drove me to the nearest emergency room, with Don and Mag in the back seat. I was given some pain medicine, stitched up and sent home. I was lucky that no major blood vessels had been cut. Actually, it felt like God was watching over me.

When we returned to the apartment, Angela was gone.

It had been an awful day, and a depressing, heavy mood filled the air. That night, everyone sat around with long faces. I felt a myriad of emotions, but mostly anger and resentment.

I was tired of being the scapegoat in the family. I was tired of being the target of my sisters anger and envy. I was tired of being a part of this family.

*It was my wrist this time, but what would it be if there was a next time?* I wondered.

I think I was starting to realize that I might need a way out.

Later, Angela came in with bandages on her wrists, and we felt sad for her. I was still angry, though. I saw Sharon go up and talk quietly to her.

The next morning, we got up and went on with business as usual.

Our family didn't talk about concerning or traumatizing events. We did our best to forget them.

Ours was a family of secrets.

We boasted about our achievements, but we kept it a secret if we failed at something, or deceived someone, or did all manner of evil.

The number one rule you didn't break was—*Don't share the family's dirty laundry.*

If you did, you would be perceived as a traitor. And in this family, traitors were shamed, ostracized, and talked about.

# 14

# Redrum

While we were all struggling to live a normal life in our apartment on Cedar Street, Sharon involved herself with two men—out in the open for the whole world to see.

Charles continued to come in and out of the apartment on a regular basis, harassing people and telling Sharon how to run her life and household.

After he was let in, Charles would stride through the apartment, scowling with every step, and make a beeline for Sharon's bedroom. He never had anything to say to us kids, and we never had anything to say to him. Nobody in the family liked him as far as I could tell—especially Sheri and Angela.

I don't know what his demeanor was when he was behind Sharon's closed bedroom door, but I know they had frequent arguments.

Their arguments could be heard outside of Sharon's bedroom even with the door closed. Charles' voice, loud and angry, thundered over Sharon's during their fights.

When his visit was over, he would leave out just the way he came in—sour-faced and unwelcome.

Then there was B.T.

Sharon had dated him before too. B.T. was pleasant, easygoing, and likable. He and Ricky's father—who was long gone—were among the few men Sharon became involved with that I didn't mind being around.

B.T. was friendly and talked to everyone and we responded in kind. I don't know anybody in the family who had a problem with him. When he came over to spend time with Sharon, he greeted us with a smile, and asked how we were doing.

When he and Sharon were together in the past—before we moved into our current apartment—she took some of us kids over to his house, where we met his daughter. She looked to be about three-years-old. She was a sweet, friendly little cherub who was the spitting image of her father. He doted on her, and I got the feeling, watching them together, that she was a daddy's girl and that B.T. was her world.

B.T. was the total opposite of Charles.

In terms of personality and physicality, they couldn't have been more different. Aside from the differences in personality, B.T. was a lot taller than Charles. Also, B.T. was lithe and in-shape, whereas Charles was scrawny.

* * *

One fateful night, B.T. and Charles came over at the same time to see Sharon. All hell broke loose as they ran into each other outside the front door. We were all inside, including Mag and Harry.

Suddenly, there was a commotion outside. We heard voices.

Sharon hurried across the living room and headed towards the front door.

Everyone in the living room looked up and turned their heads in that direction.

Sharon opened the door and looked out. "They're out there fighting with knives and guns," she said with dread in her voice.

With a start, my heart sank to my stomach.

I got up from where I was sitting and ran to the door, but Harry beat me to it.

I squeezed past Sharon and looked outside. What I saw made me recoil in horror—I saw B.T., Charles, and another man Charles had brought with him, circling each other in the street, their weapons drawn.

Harry grabbed the back of my shirt, and dragged me away as Sharon shut the door.

What happened next was pure pandemonium.

Someone got the idea that one or more of the men outside fighting were going to break the door down, come inside, and kill everyone in the apartment.

Someone ushered us into the kitchen.

We got down on the floor and started screaming!

Me, the rest of the kids in the apartment, Sharon, Angela, Harry and Mag were all down on that floor, panicking and screaming, huddled together.

Angela grabbed the nearest phone, pulled it across the floor to where she was, and managed to call 911 on speaker. She frantically told the operator what was happening outside and pleaded for them to send help.

The 911 operator, however, was unhurriedly asking questions in a nonchalant manner. She wanted more information before dispatching the police, and she and Angela started arguing.

Harry, grabbing the phone in exasperation, pleaded with the 911 operator to send help *now*.

But still, the operator insisted on getting more details first.

Harry lost his patience. "What is your name?" he demanded over the phone. "What is your operator number?!"

"I'm not going to tell you that," the operator said as we cried, whimpered, and huddled together in absolute terror on that kitchen floor.

After what seemed like an eternity, the operator agreed to send the police, and Harry hung up the phone.

A few minutes later, we heard frantic footsteps running up to the door, followed by loud banging.

Sharon crept over to the door and listened.

B.T. was on the other side, pleading.

He had been shot.

He was still able to talk at first, begging Sharon to open the door, to help him.

She was talking to him through the door. She was telling him she couldn't open it.

He slid slowly down his side of the door.

Then he slumped over and bled out.

The fight was over when the bullet struck B.T.

He walked up to our front yard and grabbed his bike.

Charles was in the getaway car driving away with the other man he had brought with him, when out of anger and pure evil, one of them took their gun and shot B.T. as he was getting on his bike to ride home.

Finally, the police arrived, along with the paramedics and an ambulance.

They immediately started working on B.T.

A crowd of people gathered outside our front door, watching as they tried to save his life.

They worked on B.T. for what seemed like a long time, but it was futile.

B.T. died that night in the ambulance.

* * *

Don came and got us so we could spend the night at his apartment and get away from what happened.

As we opened the door to leave, I will never forget what I saw—The entire porch, which had two short steps leading up to the front door, was covered in blood. So was the sidewalk in front of the steps.

It was a sea of fresh, red blood that glistened eerily in the moonlight.

The moonlight had a disquieting effect on the blood, like someone had sprinkled glitter all over it.

It felt so surreal, and so tragic.

*All that blood.*

*His life had literally bled out of him as he banged on our front door and pleaded with Sharon to help him,* I thought.

He had been outside, slumped against the cold door, on the cold porch, in the cold night air—dying—while Sharon listened on the other side of that damn door and refused to help him.

*Why didn't she open the door and help him??* my mind screamed. He was her lover after all, but most importantly he was a human being. A human being.

We were able to step over the threshold and step out onto the front lawn bypassing the bloody porch and steps as we left with a bag of clothes and some hastily grabbed toiletries.

When we got to Don's house and went to bed, it was difficult to fall asleep.

That night, and for years afterward, I thought about B.T. dropping his bike as he was shot, breathlessly running up to our door for help, and then dying against it as Sharon rejected him.

I thought about his daughter, who would now have to grow up without the father that loved her so much. That little girl was his world, and he was hers.

Now, they would never see each other again, at least on this earth. It was very sad.

Two days later we came back to the apartment and tried to get back to normal.

Although she would never admit it, Sharon had to know she was responsible for B.T.'s death.

Her guilt seeped out in strange ways: She acted out and demonstrated with her hands and body how B.T. must have slid slowly down the door as the blood flowed out of his body.

She was listening, and she had heard him dying.

It's painful to imagine the panic and the horror he must have felt as his life was slipping away, as he resigned himself to the fact that Sharon wasn't going to open the door and come to his aid.

Later, Sharon blamed B.T. for his own death, claiming he wasted his energy banging on the door instead of waiting calmly for help. Her logic was as warped as her denial.

I marveled at how delusional she was. *Had she really gaslit herself into believing what she was saying?* I wondered.

I looked down, refusing to meet her eyes as she rambled on. I didn't want her to see the disapproval in mine.

Next, she attributed his murder to a framed picture hanging on the living room wall—a close-up of a casket spray atop a casket. She said she had been meaning to take it down and throw it in the trash bin because she thought it was cursed.

She explained that she kept looking at the picture, trying to figure out what it was supposed to be, since the close-up of the floral arrangement made it difficult to tell it was resting on a casket. When she finally realized what it depicted, she knew it had to go.

*The only curse in this house was her*, I thought, guilt creeping in as she rambled on. She had to be suffering to some extent because no matter how many times she was wont to deny it, she had to know she was at fault.

Sharon never faced the truth: her lover murdered B.T. and she was complicit because she was involved with both men at the same time. It wasn't because of some creepy picture hanging on her wall. Denial was her savior, letting her bury the blame and walk away—innocent in her own eyes.

But, in no one else's.

# 15

## Sharon's Shame

There was significant fallout after B.T.'s murder, most of which was justified. As expected, his family was devastated. They wanted justice, and they wanted revenge.

One day B.T.'s brother came over and stood outside of our apartment. He saw Sheri standing nearby. Scowling, he pointed to our concrete front porch and asked her, "Is this where my brother died?"

"He died in the ambulance," Sheri replied. Which may or may not have been true. She quickly came into the house and told us what happened. Sharon congratulated her on how she handled it.

None of us knew when B.T.'s heart had stopped—on the porch, in the ambulance, or at the hospital. All I knew was they worked on him in the ambulance before transporting him to the hospital. We watched through the living room blinds inside the apartment that awful night.

In any event, Sheri's answer wasn't intended to tell B.T's brother the truth. It was intended to assuage his anger and protect her mother. *Ah, yes, protect her mother*, I thought. She would always protect her mother in any situation, even if she had to lie. And when it came to her mother, she lied. A lot.

She was always and forever her mother's number one propagandist and flying monkey. She was the one who would hide the empty alcohol bottles when her mother started drinking heavily after she got off the drugs later in life.

Charles and his accomplice were both arrested and taken into custody, and after a while, there was a trial. I don't know who actually pulled the trigger, but they were both guilty.

When it came time for Charles' trial, Sharon was subpoenaed, and she dutifully appeared in court. She went alone at first, then one day she came home flustered and upset and explained to us that B.T.'s family had run up to where Charles was sitting at the defendant's table and attacked him.

By Sharon's account, all hell broke loose in the courtroom that day. They jumped on Charles, pummeled him with their fists, kicked him, and did whatever they could to take their hurt and pain out on him for killing their beloved brother, uncle, cousin, etc.

Eventually order was restored in the courtroom, and Sharon came home that day scared she was going to be next. It was a valid fear because of her terrible actions that lead to the confrontation between the two men in the first place.

I was surprised that some of B.T.'s family didn't attack her at the same time they attacked Charles. Nevertheless, Mag made sure Don accompanied her to the courtroom from then on.

Before and all throughout the trial, there was an air of unease among those of us in the apartment because we knew B.T.'s family was very angry. Their primary target would be Sharon, of course, but we didn't know what they might do or if any of us could be hurt in the crossfire.

Don was a frequent visitor to the apartment, more so when Mag and Harry arrived from Chicago because he wanted to be around our mother.

He did go home to Audrey at night, but he would come over and visit Mag as much as he could, which was usually every other day. Sometimes, he would spend the night on her and Harry's couch when we got our own place. A lot of times, Audrey came over with him.

One day, he came over to our apartment with some frightening news regarding our mother. We looked at him in astonishment as he told us he heard there was a contract out on Mag's life.

*A contract,* I thought.*Why?* Mag didn't like what she heard either; fear and worry flashed quickly across her face, which turned red and ugly.

*Who would put a contract out on somebody's elderly mother who hadn't even done anything?* I thought. I didn't know whether to laugh or cry because it was so ridiculous. I would have thought the contract would have been on Sharon. Maybe there was one out on her too.

The news of the contract on Mag was very worrisome to all of us. The unfortunate news added another layer of tension to what was already a tense and anxiety-ridden environment due to the murder and trial.

I don't know if it was talked about further after that. If it was, I wasn't part of the discussion. I just kept hoping it wasn't true and that it would all blow over without any harm coming to Mag. We waited apprehensively for something to happen, and breathed a sigh of relief when the threat never materialized.

Just when I thought Sharon couldn't sink any lower, what happened next shocked everyone in the apartment. We started noticing that she was putting on weight, and her clothes were getting tighter and tighter around the stomach area. We began whispering among each other, following her discreetly with our eyes when she would enter and leave the apartment. I was reluctant to put into words what everyone was thinking.

*Nah, it couldn't be,* I thought. *She couldn't be that stupid. Could she?*

Yes, she was *that* stupid. Of course, Sheri was told before the rest of us. When Sharon couldn't hide it any longer, she came inside the house one day and dropped a bomb on us—She was pregnant. By Charles. The murderer.

My jaw literally dropped. Our inaudible gasps reverberated around the room, bounced off the walls, and landed squarely at Sharon's feet.

I stared at her, desperately trying to hide my revulsion. Her eyes looked big and hollow. I noticed she had started wearing her hair like her daughter's, parted in the middle with a French braid on both sides. It looked childish. I dropped my eyes. None of us said a word. What was there to say? Besides, none of us wanted to risk her flying into one of her unhinged rages.

I looked over at our mother. She looked sad and defeated. Everyone was extremely disappointed in Sharon. She already had two kids by two different men who were not in her kids' life, and this baby would make number three.

*Three strikes and you're out,* I couldn't help thinking.

The silver lining was maybe the pregnancy would keep her off drugs—at least for the next nine months. There were no guarantees, but I was keeping my fingers crossed.

After we got over the initial shock of the pregnancy announcement, none of us wanted to admit what we were all thinking: Was the baby Charles'? B.T.'s? *Or somebody else's entirely...?*

After all, Sharon had been promiscuous the whole time I had been in California—and probably before. She continued to assert that she was pregnant by Charles, so we had no choice but to take her word for it.

Nine months later she gave birth to the murderer's baby.

It was a boy who looked very much like his father. She named him Asion and gave him his father's last name. It wasn't the baby's fault that he was born into these circumstances. He didn't choose his parents or their actions, but he became a living reminder of a painful time.

# 16

# Behind Sharon's Shadow

Eventually, Mag, Harry, and I moved out of Sharon's apartment and into a one-bedroom apartment directly behind hers in the same building.

Whereas Sharon's apartment faced the street, our apartment sat at a right angle to hers, and our front door faced a semi-narrow courtyard that was partially enclosed by a wooden fence.

Angela moved out of state with her son, and Anton moved into our apartment with us a few weeks later.

Mag and Harry had the bedroom, and Anton and I slept on the two couches in the living room. It was a far cry from our standard of living in Chicago. I was frustrated, but realized there was nothing I could do about it.

I was hoping Harry would start working soon, or they would start over and open a restaurant in California, but those hopes were dashed when Mag reluctantly explained that Harry was conflicted about doing either because he owed the IRS money.

*Wow! That's just great,* I thought. With no money coming in, I was confused as to how they could afford the rent. I was so disillusioned, I didn't even ask. I thought they must have money saved up somewhere.

I realized this particular apartment was chosen because the rent was cheap, and it was close to Sharon's apartment. Also, it was convenient for Mag whenever Sharon needed her to baby sit. The close proximity allowed for both adults and kids to circulate frequently among the apartments.

Anton moved in with us because he had nowhere else to go. He was heavily on drugs. Harry objected because of his drug problem, but Mag was incapable of saying no to Anton.

He was her absolute favorite, and she didn't bother hiding it. Her other two sons came next, and her daughters were last. I discovered this early on, but I wasn't really bothered by it because I was my father's favorite, so I really didn't need her affection—so I thought.

Both our parents strictly forbade Anton from using drugs in or around our apartment. They didn't want it around them, me, or any of their grandchildren, plus it was illegal.

By the time they arrived in California, Sharon was supposedly weening herself off the drugs and trying to rebuild her life. I hadn't yet told them how the rest of their kids were into drugs before they arrived—and how much us kids suffered because of it—but they would soon find out on their own.

On the calls home when they were back in Chicago, Sharon talked first and made everything seem rosy before putting me on the phone.

She made it a habit to be near the phone when I talked to them, sometimes even standing over me. I knew without being told that she did not want me to tell on any of them.

Then, after I talked, she would get on the phone and gaslight them some more—then gaslight me when she got off.

I was so relieved we had moved out, and I would no longer be under Sharon's foot.

# 17

## Prison Didn't Change Him

With all of us gone, that left room for Charles to move directly into Sharon's apartment upon his release from prison, which was exactly what he did.

Fresh out of prison, Charles stepped right back into Sharon's, their new baby's, and unfortunately, our lives too. He was the same old Charles—mean and unfriendly to everyone around him.

I didn't see the slightest flicker of remorse or sorrow in his face for what he had done to B.T. Nor did he apologize to us for what he had put us all through that night.

Charles was indifferent to the baby. Sharon would try to push him off on Charles in the hopes that Charles would develop a close connection with the baby. She encouraged Charles to hold him, feed him, and change his diaper.

Charles would do these things occasionally, but it quickly became apparent that he wasn't going to be anything close to a model father.

Nevertheless, Sharon and Charles got married. I assumed it was a courthouse affair because no one I knew was invited to either a wedding or a reception.

One day, she came home sporting a wedding ring set and announced they were married. She was gushing and blushing like a young bride. "Charles said his vows so softly," she chattered on.

*Could it have been because he really didn't want to marry you?* I thought, with a good measure of guilt. I hastily pushed the thought out of my mind.

Of course, no one in the family was happy about it. We all knew what kind of man Charles was. So did she, and yet she had married him anyway.

One day, on the way home, I passed by Sharon's apartment as I walked on the other side of the street. Her blinds were open, and I observed a confrontation unfold between her and Charles that almost turned violent. It had just gotten dark, and I could easily see into their lit front room. There were bushes in front of the window, so I hoped they wouldn't be able to see me looking in their direction even if they looked out.

There was no need to worry, as they were busy concentrating on the meal they were getting ready to eat, sitting on the coffee table.

It was a pot of pinto beans with ground beef.

Not a good cook by any means, Charles had a couple of favorite dishes that he made over and over again. Those were pinto beans with ground beef, and barbecue pork ribs. He liked his ribs burned to a crisp. He loved them, but they were difficult for others to eat.

It was only Sharon, Charles, and their son Asion. She served them up bowls of the beans and sat down to enjoy her meal. Asion was learning to walk, and he was pulling himself around the coffee table as he sampled food from his bowl and theirs.

Sharon and Charles starting arguing.

Suddenly, they both stood up abruptly and faced each other. I watched through the window as Charles balled up his fist, brought it near Sharon's face, and started threatening her with it. Her head snapped back, and she walked around the coffee table and left the room.

I quickly walked on, crossing the street after I passed their window. I walked pass the driveway into the courtyard, and finally into the apartment I shared with my parents.

* * *

Charles secured a job at the shipyard and was making good money. Another bonus: he was paid weekly. Sharon had big plans for that money. First on the list was saving for a down payment on a house.

Every Friday, when Charles got paid, they treated themselves to their favorite Chinese restaurant. One afternoon, I was outside near the apartment building when Sharon and Sheri came up to me, looking for Ricky. Charles had just gotten home from work, and they were getting ready to go.

I perked up at the mention of the restaurant. They'd never invited me to go with them, even though they went every weekend. 'That sounds delicious,' I said with a hopeful smile. My mind filled with images of steaming dumplings and fragrant stir-fry, glistening in savory sauces.

They looked at me like I was dirt.

My smile disappeared. *What the fuck?!* I thought as I stared at them, confusion tightening my chest. I couldn't figure out what I'd done to deserve the look on their faces.

They turned away and kept looking for Ricky. I went back into my apartment, feeling dejected. A little while later, I heard them find Ricky and leave for the Chinese restaurant.

A short time later, they moved out of their apartment and into another building not that far away. I could see why they would do that. Charles didn't like anybody in Sharon's family, and he wouldn't want to live so close to them.

They moved to their new apartment and tried to live a happy life, but pretty soon, cracks began to emerge. Sharon and Mag liked to talk and gossip, so they'd visit each other's apartment regularly. Usually, Sharon would just come over to our apartment.

One day, she came over with a rambling story about how long Charles takes in the shower and how the steam can be seen outside the bathroom. I sat there on the couch, wondering when she was going to get to the point.

She seemed jovial, but I got the feeling she was really complaining about something she didn't like. *Was there a point to all this? Or was she just filling the air with nonsense to avoid saying what she really meant?*

Soon, word started swirling around the family gossip mill that Sharon and Charles were having trouble in their marriage. Rumor had it Charles was now spending most of his paycheck on drugs.

They struggled along for a while, but ultimately, they couldn't make the marriage work. Sharon pulled the plug by moving out.

Charles didn't take the news well. He came outside and threatened the few people that Sharon had gathered to help her move with a knife.

When the divorce was final, and all was said and done, most of the family breathed a sigh of relief—Charles was out of our lives.

Or so we thought.

# 18

# Angela's Mess, Our Stress

One day, Angela returned from out of state pregnant, with her son and a new boyfriend. His name was Glenn, and I wasn't sure if she introduced him as her boyfriend or fiancé. I didn't remember seeing a ring, though she could have had one. She looked to be about six or seven months along.

They moved in with us in the one-bedroom apartment my parents had rented, bringing the total number of occupants to seven, not counting the baby.

Glenn was on the thin side, but he was nice-looking and respectful. I liked him immediately. He could hold a conversation, and he had a calm, even voice. He was an upgrade from the men she had been with before she left California.

I was rooting for them, thinking that if this one works out, it could be a good thing. The new baby would have a live-in father.

Still wary of Angela and the violence she inflicted on me before she left, I avoided engaging with her and tried to stay out of her way. I didn't hold a grudge, but I wasn't eager to be in her presence either.

As far as her attacking me, the subject never came up. She didn't apologize or explain her actions, and I didn't bring it up either. My parents never attempted to obtain counseling for me concerning Angela's assaults, which didn't seem right to me.

*Don't air the family's dirty laundry*, a mocking voice sang in my head.

Ours was definitely a family that kept secrets. Bad secrets. Secrets of things they'd done to hurt people inside and outside the family.

We dealt with Angela and Glenn as best we could. As the months rolled by, it became increasingly difficult. There were several hiccups.

One day, I was in the kitchen in front of a pot of boiling water, preparing to make macaroni and cheese from a box. Suddenly, Angela came up behind me, pushed me aside, and took over stirring the pot.

"This needs more milk, more cheese, and more butter. The way to a man's heart is through his stomach," she said in her loud, boisterous voice, dripping with rancid honey.

This was when I first realized that Angela was desperate to keep Glenn from leaving her.

While I stared at her in disbelief, Don spoke up from the living room behind us, "Angela, that's not right."

Don didn't usually like to get involved, but I guess Angela's behavior was so beyond the pale that he had to say something.

A flicker of emotion flashed across her face, but I couldn't tell what it was. I turned and walked away, letting her cook the macaroni and cheese.

Angela and Glenn seemed to get along fine—until one event made me wonder if trouble was brewing.

One day, not knowing anyone was watching me that closely, I bent over to take something out of the oven while wearing snug-fitting jeans. Suddenly, from somewhere in the room behind me, Glenn called out, "Buttah!"

Angela's harsh voice cut across the air immediately. "Glenn!" she cried out. "How could you?" she said in a wounded voice.

Glenn just shrugged, and they went on with their day. I went on with mine as well, without further incident.

A few months later, Angela gave birth to a baby girl she and Glenn named British.

The baby was healthy—as far as I knew—and I hoped she would motivate Angela to work harder at being a good mother to both of her kids. *Eddie deserved so much more than she was giving him.*

# 19

# Kool-Aid and Chaos

I wasn't brought up religiously. My parents didn't talk about church or pray at home in my presence. Harry was a non-practicing Catholic. He probably didn't remember the last time he stepped inside a Catholic Church to attend Mass.

His mother and two sisters, and probably his two brothers, were Catholic as well. The only time Mag and Harry took me to church was once a year on Easter Sunday when I was a little girl in Chicago.

One day, Evan, the boy I had started dating down the street, invited my family and I to a local Baptist church that he and his family attended.

After a few services, we were hooked, especially my father.We enjoyed the sermons and fell in love with the church's pastor. He was like King David, a man after God's own heart.

Most of us accepted Christ as our Savior and joined the church. My father became extremely dedicated to our pastor and was at the church several nights a week. It wasn't long before Harry was made a deacon.

The Church became a needed distraction from our living situation at home, which had steadily gone down hill since Angela, Glenn, and Anton moved in.

Anton's drug use had gotten worse, and it was obvious that Angela and Glenn were using drugs as well.

This caused almost constant arguments between my parents. Harry wanted Mag to put her foot down and tell them all to leave, but she just couldn't, especially when it came to Anton.

My youngest brother was a rebel who often broke the rules, but he would charm the pants off you so you couldn't stay mad at him. That seemed to work with most of the family, but not me.

I was plenty mad at Anton for all the trouble he was causing our family, and I resented the way my mother excused everything wrong he did. Still, I loved him dearly, and I really wanted him to get help for his addiction because he had struggled with it for a long time.

Plus, he needed to be a full-time father instead of a part-time one to his three daughters, Tammi, Nichole, and Marnya.

Mag and Harry continued to warn Angela, Anton, and Glenn not to bring drugs into the apartment or use them on the premises.

Also, Harry didn't want them coming in and out of the apartment after midnight. To get around that, they began creeping around and climbing in and out of the windows at all hours of the night.

Sometimes, we would be fast asleep when we would be abruptly woken up by one or more of them sneaking in through the living room window.

Mag began to crack up. The tension and chaos in the apartment were starting to get to her. The worse Angela, Anton, and Glenn messed up, the angrier and more depressed she became.

One day, angry at something somebody said, she went into the kitchen, took out a pitcher of red Kool-Aid, and preceded to fling it all over the walls.

Harry ran into the kitchen and tried to take the pitcher out of her hands.

"Stop! Stop!" he roared! "I don't want to have to clean all this mother-fucking sticky ass shit off the walls!"

Fury glittering in her eyes, Mag defiantly flung the rest of what was left in the pitcher on the walls, dropped it on the floor, and stormed out of the kitchen.

I think the stress of it all was what made my mother start drinking heavily again. Once again, my mother turned to the bottle to ease the pain and depression of life's disappointments, just like she had back in Chicago when they loss both the house and business.

I helplessly watched her go downhill, unable to do anything about it.

\* \* \*

I had started attending classes at Long Beach City College. I hadn't decided on a concrete career path yet, so I was taking general education classes until I figured it out.

I came home from school one day to find Angela nervously standing by the door with a guilty look on her face.

I heard Anton's voice coming from the bathroom—there was a direct view to the bathroom from the front door. I dropped my book bag on the couch and turned towards the bathroom to see what was going on.

To my absolute horror, Glenn was passed out in the bathtub, fully dressed, with shower water streaming down on him, soaking his clothes.

Anton was standing over him, slapping him in the face and frantically trying to revive him.

By this time, Angela had grabbed the phone and taken the handset off in preparation to call emergency services. I looked at her angrily and said, "What are you waiting for?"

I grabbed the phone and immediately called 911.

Several cops arrived and stormed through the apartment toward the bathroom. A couple of them went in, saw what was going on, grabbed Glenn, and started slapping and shaking him, saying things like, "Hey, buddy, wake up!"

Once Glenn was revived, they filed out of the apartment, looking just as angry as they had when they came in.

As they were leaving, they looked disgusted, glancing around noting the unkempt apartment with the dirty carpeting.

One of them disrespectfully remarked, "He's okay now. He just had a little too much crack".

I was deeply offended by this statement. They were supposed to help people. They were hired to serve and protect, and I saw no reason for the disrespect.

Standing over by the front door, which was now completely open, I said, "I'm not a part of this."

A belligerent cop looked at me sardonically and said, "Sure you're not" as he swaggered out the door.

That hurt. The last thing I wanted was to be associated with criminal activity.

*Couldn't they see I was a minor and not involved in this mess?* I wondered desperately.

I wanted to defend myself and say more, but I kept my mouth shut because I didn't want them to turn on me.

In my mind, I struggled to reconcile their behavior with the fact that they were obviously tired and frustrated because they were called out to this apartment complex, and street, often because of all the crime that took place here.

Still, their statements and behavior made me feel both disrespected and bullied, and this caused me to have a deep resentment of law enforcement for many, many years.

I came home one day to find out that our neighbor Melanie, who lived in the apartment on the other side of ours, had been robbed the previous night. Somebody stole eight hundred dollars from underneath her mattress, and she was sure that Anton and Glenn had done it.

Anton and Glenn had gone over her apartment under false pretenses to wine and dine her. They created a party atmosphere, plied Melanie with alcohol, and possibly drugs, and played her like a violin.

As the alcohol, and possibly drugs, flowed freely, her tongue became looser and looser. Before the night was over, she made the mistake of telling them she had saved up a large sum of money and kept it under her bed.

Anton and Glenn wasted no time. They broke into her apartment the next day and stole her money while she was at work.

When Melanie came home from work, we heard her screaming on the other side of our wall when she discovered her eight hundred dollars was gone.

Of course, Melanie knew it had been Anton and Glenn. She told us later that they were the only ones she had told where the money was hidden.

Angela was ever-present, hanging around in the shadows, and barely taking care of her newborn daughter and her son. Eddie was spending a lot of time over Sharon's house because he was close with Ricky.

Mag, a decent woman who cared about what happened to people, was sad and upset when she found out what Anton and Glenn had done to Melanie.

However, she couldn't bare to put Anton out, so Angela and Glenn stayed too.

Mag saw Melanie coming out of her apartment one day and ran up to her. They both hugged each other and cried about what had happened. Melanie stood there and sobbed on Mag's bosom, saying how reprehensible it was for people to deceive others and steal their money.

Mag agreed and tried her best to comfort her. Of course, she couldn't get the money back for Melanie—Mag knew it was long gone, having already been spent on drugs.

That was the last time Melanie spoke to Mag or anyone else in our apartment again. She walked past us with her head either down or pointed straight ahead. Soon, she packed up her things and moved away with her young daughter.

* * *

While all this was going on, Sharon had seemingly given up drugs and appeared to be trying to get her life together again.

She was guilty of how she had cruelly neglected me and her children, and her other crimes against humanity that ruined lives and left bodies in the street.

But she desperately worked to change the narrative to make it look like she was innocent of everything.

For that, being the malignant narcissist that she was, she needed to assign dysfunctional roles to other members of the family to support her delusion that she was blameless.

What Sheri hadn't realized at first, but denied later on when she did realize it, was that she was but a puppet on a string, controlled by an evil marionette she called, "mom."

She was forever expected to do Sharon's bidding, even when that meant hurting other members of the family.

There was no escaping this role either, as long as she wanted to remain in Sharon's good graces. Like me, she had been given a lifetime sentence.

But Sharon, full of evil intent, also needed a scapegoat who she could deflect blame onto. That way, she could look at herself in the mirror, and not see the *real* Sharon looking back at her. And, make no mistake, the real Sharon was deeply flawed, mentally unstable, and *very* dangerous.

For the role of scapegoat, Sharon looked around, and her eyes fell on the most vulnerable member of the family. Her old faithful—Me. She wasn't going to choose her son, Ricky, for she loved him too much.

I suspected, as did Sheri's husband Lance later on when she married, that Ricky was the child Sharon loved far more than the others. She worked real hard to hide it, but it came out in trickles, dribbles, and tidbits of information. And if you paid close enough attention, you could detect it.

But she couldn't let Sheri know and risk losing her puppet because Ricky wasn't going to take her place. He was his own person, and her only child who would stand up to her and call her out on her behavior.

I think Ricky saw in his mother what his father saw in her before he bailed— and he wasn't going to lie for her, or function as her puppet, or flying monkey.

Ricky, who resented how much Sharon neglected them, and how she let Anton whip him when she was overwhelmed and working, would curse her out to her face, calling her names like "Bitch"—and get away with it.

He railed against her for her drug use and how she had been a terrible mother. He told her how he and her other kids had witnessed atrocities that they never should have seen. She couldn't deny it. He was right on all accounts.

And while she gaslighted everyone one else, she didn't attempt to gaslight Ricky because he wasn't going for it—and she knew that.

So, Sharon really needed a scapegoat, and unfortunately, she chose me. Her grudges and vendettas against me reinforced her delusional belief that I was the enemy.

By the time we were living with her in the front apartment, she had effectively turned Sheri against me and was working on Ricky.

Also, unbeknownst to me, she had already been setting the stage to turn both Mag and Harry, my own parents, against me as well.

# 20

# Impact

I kept seeing the boy down the street, and over time, a relationship developed. But we were two very different people, and things gradually began to fall apart.

One day, Evan was driving me around in his mother's car since he didn't have his own yet. We started arguing, and he accidentally drove the car into a traffic signal.

The car seemed to approach the traffic signal in slow motion.

Then, impact.

I blacked out.

When I came to, everything was a blur, and blood was dripping down my face. I looked down and saw that my legs were wedged partly under the dashboard, and my thigh was bent. Neither one of us were wearing our seat belt.

I looked over at Evan who was leaning over the steering wheel. He was dazed too, and his jaw looked distorted. He started crying and whimpering in pain, hitting the steering wheel in frustration.

I felt so bad for him; it was obvious he was badly hurt and in serious pain.

Suddenly, I heard the faint cry of sirens that grew steadily louder.

A crowd had gathered outside the car. People were looking into the windows, and calling out, "Help is on the way! Help is on the way!" It seemed like just moments later paramedics and the police arrived.

The paramedics quickly loaded Evan and me onto stretchers and rushed us to Long Beach Memorial Hospital in separate ambulances.

When we arrived, doctors and nurses were waiting for us at the emergency room entrance. They whisked us inside and into examination rooms.

Inside the hospital, there was a whirlwind of activity around me. I could hear hospital noises—staff hustling and bustling through the corridors, and doctors being paged over the PA system.

After I was examined, staff wheeled my bed out into the hallway, presumably to wait on an operating room to become available. I could no longer see my leg which was now covered by a sheet, but I could feel the sticky blood all over my face.

I was trying to figure out how badly I was hurt when Mag and Harry came rushing up to my bed, with Don hot on their heels.

Mag took one look at me and became visibly upset. She started wringing her hands and crying. They left to find one of the nurses or doctors to get more information.

Before long, they came back.

While they were gone, a nurse came over and began writing something on a chart.

Don turned toward her and asked, "Can you wipe the blood off of her face?"

She ignored him, finished writing on her chart, and quickly walked away.

Don called after her, "Can somebody please wipe the blood off her face? It's upsetting her mother!"

I believe Don went into one of the restrooms, came back with some dampened paper towels, and wiped my face himself. I wasn't bothered by the blood on my face, but he didn't want Mag upset.

Soon, I was taken upstairs and into a surgery room.

They gently transferred me to the surgery table and prepared me for surgery.

I turned my attention to the anesthesiologist, who had started administering the anesthesia in a soft, soothing voice. He directed me to count back from 100.

I did so in my mind, and before I could get to 90, I was out.

* * *

I woke up in a darkened, quiet recovery room to see my leg in a sling and Mag, Harry, and Don sitting at the foot of my bed.

I had sustained a superficial cut on my forehead and a broken left femur.

Evan's family was also at the hospital, and they told my family that Evan's jaw was broken but he was going to be okay.

I breathed a sigh of relief and thought how lucky I was to be alive.

When it was time to leave the recovery room, staff wheeled my bed into an elevator and took me to another wing of the hospital.

From there, they wheeled me into my new hospital room where I would remain for the next several months while my leg healed.

* * *

I became used to my new surroundings fairly quickly. I had my own TV, three healthy, tasty meals a day—complete with milk, juice, dessert—and nurses waiting on me hand and foot.

I needed them, of course, since I could no longer stand up or walk. My bed was right next to a big window that let the sunlight in during the day and the moonlight in at night.

I was given morphine for the pain, which I really didn't feel until it was time for my next dose.

I was astounded at how well morphine worked. It kept me out of pain and extremely comfortable.

Mag and Don visited my room one day, and the nurse came in to give me my morphine pill. She handed me the pill and a cup of water and stood there while I took it. She looked formidable and in charge. She was *not* leaving my room until I swallowed it, especially with people around.

I took the morphine pill, and as it took effect, a dreamy haze settled over me. It felt like I was swirling in my own personal funnel cloud—multi-colored, and only about six feet tall, floating inside my hospital room.

I became even dreamier.

"I'm falling..." I sang.

Don chuckled as Mag looked on. Before I knew it, I had fallen into a very pleasant sleep.

\* \* \*

I spent my time in my hospital room reading, working crossword puzzles, journaling, and watching TV.

I liked it when visitors came to see me. Some even brought beautiful flowers and get-well cards.

I especially enjoyed it when a youth minister from our church came to visit and brought some young adults from the youth choir. They brought cards and a bouquet of flowers, and it really made me happy. I felt loved and valued.

When Evan's jaw had healed enough, his nurses and doctors allowed him to come down in a wheelchair to visit. His jaw was wired shut, but the visits were pleasant, and I was relieved he had survived the accident.

We didn't talk about the accident. I just wanted to put it behind me and heal.

Mag, however, refused to file a claim against Evan's mother's car insurance company because they were friends. To my utter irritation, she never asked my opinion—she simply made the decision for me.

But, it wasn't her decision to make.

I wasn't happy about it because it wasn't a good business decision.

Mag and Harry would continue their controlling ways when I left the hospital, which made me want to move away from them as soon as was practical.

\* \* \*

My orthopedic surgeon came by regularly to check on my leg. He had put a steel rod in it to stabilize the bone as it healed. He explained that he would remove it at some point after I left the hospital.

One day, the physical therapist came in my room. It was time for me to begin trying to walk on my leg.

I inched over to the side of the bed, and she helped me cautiously stand up.

I put a little weight on it, and the pain shot up my leg like lightning.

*It hurt like hell!*

I sat back down, exhausted and perspiring. The physical therapist helped me push myself back onto the bed.

"That's enough for one day," she said.

I breathed a sigh of relief.

She left, and I reclined back and clicked on the TV. I was getting hungry, and it was almost time for lunch. It was also time for my next dose of medication, and I sure needed it—my leg was throbbing.

* * *

A few days later, the physical therapist returned and worked with me again. We set a regular schedule, and over the next few weeks, I slowly regained my leg strength—first with a walker, then crutches.

Eventually, I was able to walk down the hall with assistance.

One day, my doctor came by and said I was well enough to go home.

By the end of that week, I had checked out and was wheeled downstairs to the lobby to wait for Mag and Harry to pick me up.

I had mixed feelings about going home. I knew I couldn't stay in the hospital forever, but going back to Cedar Street—and the problems Angela, Glenn, and Anton had brought into our lives—wasn't something I was looking forward to.

On the short drive home, I half-listened to Mag and Harry's chatter, but I wasn't really paying attention. I was thinking about our home life, wondering if anything had changed for the better since I'd been gone.

As Harry's car pulled into a parking space in front of our apartment, I gritted my teeth and hoped for the best.

# The Seven Deadly Sins and How My Betrayers Committed Each One

The people who destroyed me—**Sharon, Sheri, Angela, and Dr. Lance Robert**—are guilty of all seven deadly sins, even though they portray themselves as God-fearing Christians. However, **true Christians don't behave like that**. Their betrayal wasn't just cruel; it was **the ultimate moral failing.**

1. **Pride** – They believed they were **untouchable**, superior, and justified in their actions. They refused to **admit wrongdoing**, even in the face of undeniable proof. Their **egos** wouldn't allow them to take accountability.

2. **Greed** – Lance, in particular, played a major role in my destruction **for money**. They aligned themselves with my abusive ex-husband because it benefited them **financially**. They valued **wealth and comfort** over my well-being, my rights as a mother, and my children's happiness.

3. **Wrath** – Sharon, Sheri, and Angela's deep-seated **resentment** toward me fueled their **ruthless** and **calculated** betrayal. Their **vindictiveness knew no bounds**, and they destroyed my life with deliberate malice.

4. **Envy** – Sharon and Angela were **envious** of my relationship with my father, **who loved me more than them**. Their jealousy poisoned their hearts and led them to **orchestrate my downfall**.

5. **Lust** – Sharon's **reckless and wanton** behavior led to chaos and destruction,

not only in my life but in the lives of others. Her choices had devastating consequences for everyone around her.

6. **Gluttony** – They wanted **more—more power, more control, more dominance**. It wasn't enough to see me struggle; they wanted to **erase me completely** and consume **everything I had left**.

7. **Sloth** – They avoided **responsibility** for their actions. Even when confronted with the pain they caused, they chose to **do nothing** rather than make amends. Their **cowardice and inaction** spoke louder than any words ever could.

# DOCUMENTED EVIDENCE

In this section, I present key documents and communications that support the events and claims discussed in this book. These pieces of evidence provide transparency and authenticity to the narrative. The following pages contain official documents and personal text message exchanges that further illustrate the betrayal, manipulation, and injustices I endured.

**Official Documents**

**Letter from My Father to the Court**

**Date: June 23, 2008**

**Summary:**

My father wrote this letter during my custody battle in response to Sharon and Angela's letters to the judge urging him to take my children away. In it, he exposes Sharon's history of deception and manipulation, as well as the reckless behavior of both sisters. This letter is undeniable proof that my parents knew the truth about their daughters and their intent to harm me. He put it in writing for the court to see.

5:13 PM   Mon Apr 18                                                                    65%

🔒 epublic-access.riverside.courts.ca.gov

MC-030

| ATTORNEY OR PARTY WITHOUT ATTORNEY (Name, State Bar number, and address): | FOR COURT USE ONLY |
|---|---|
| TELEPHONE NO.:          FAX NO. (Optional): | |
| E-MAIL ADDRESS (Optional): | |
| ATTORNEY FOR (Name): | |

**SUPERIOR COURT OF CALIFORNIA, COUNTY OF**
STREET ADDRESS:
MAILING ADDRESS:
CITY AND ZIP CODE:
BRANCH NAME:

PLAINTIFF/PETITIONER:

DEFENDANT/RESPONDENT:

**DECLARATION**

CASE NUMBER:

7. It hurts me to present this to the court, but I believe that my daughter Sharon Malum is a pathological liar. She has told damaging lies to both me and her mother. She is a former drug addict and has abused both illegal street drugs and alcohol during the youthful period in which she was raising her children.

8. My daughter Angela has a criminal record, she is a convicted felon and a former drug addict. I believe that Angela is abusing prescription drugs prescribed to her to her cancer diagnosis. I have witnessed Angela falling asleep right in the middle of a conversation.

9. Angela cut Marion on her wrist during a period of anger when she was younger.

10. The court should not consider any statements by Angela & Sharon regarding Marion Palmer highly suspect.

I declare under penalty of perjury under the laws of the State of California that the foregoing is true and correct.

Date: 6-23-08 Harry Droke

_____
(TYPE OR PRINT NAME)

*Harry Duke*
(SIGNATURE OF DECLARANT)

☐ Attorney for  ☐ Plaintiff  ☐ Petitioner  ☐ Defendant
☐ Respondent  ☐ Other (Specify):

**DECLARATION**

Page 1 of 1

# Letter from My Mother to the Court

# Date: June 23, 2008

**Summary:**

In this letter, my mother outlines my sisters' plot against me. She goes into further detail about the damage caused by Sharon and Angela, and also reveals Sheri's brainwashing of my sons, making it clear that their actions had devastating consequences. This document further discredits the false accusations that were used to justify taking my children away from me.

MC-030

ATTORNEY OR PARTY WITHOUT ATTORNEY *(Name, State Bar number, and address)*:

FOR COURT USE ONLY

TELEPHONE NO.          FAX NO. *(Optional)*:
E-MAIL ADDRESS *(Optional)*:
ATTORNEY FOR *(Name)*:

SUPERIOR COURT OF CALIFORNIA, COUNTY OF
STREET ADDRESS:
MAILING ADDRESS:
CITY AND ZIP CODE:
BRANCH NAME:

PLAINTIFF/PETITIONER:

DEFENDANT/RESPONDENT:

CASE NUMBER:

**DECLARATION**

I am the mother of Marion Palmer and I agree with both the declarations made by my husband, Harry Drake during his statements

Marion was not aware that her sisters were going to set her up making false allegations against her and aid Steven Palmer in his attempts to take the children away from her. Marion was not even aware that the declarations made by Sharon and Angela even existed the morning of June 12, right before she entered the courtroom. They were filed that morning and Steven Palmer had them served on her when she entered the courtroom in Hemet Ca.

I am asking the court to please not take custody away from my daughter, she is a very good mother.

I believe that my granddaughter have attempted to brainwash my grand sons and turn him against his own mother.

I declare under penalty of perjury under the laws of the State of California that the foregoing is true and correct.

Date: 6-23-08   Maggie Drake

_____
(TYPE OR PRINT NAME)

*Maggie Drake*
(SIGNATURE OF DECLARANT)

☐ Attorney for  ☐ Plaintiff  ☐ Petitioner  ☐ Defendant
☐ Respondent  ☐ Other *(Specify)*:

Form Approved for Optional Use
Judicial Council of California
MC-030 [Rev. January 1, 2006]

**DECLARATION**

Page 1 of 1

American LegalNet, Inc.
www.USCourtForms.com

# Text Message Evidence

## Conversation with Angela: Lance's Manipulation & Betrayal

**Date: March 26, 2024**

**Summary:**

In this message, Angela admits that she was approached by Lance to give a false statement against me. She acknowledges that she wasn't thinking clearly and that she had no idea what was really happening when she agreed to betray me. Angela also reveals that Sheri manipulated her into believing my children would be staying with family, not with Steve. This was a lie as well, since my children were going to remain with me, where they belonged.

Her confession exposes Lance's direct role in orchestrating the false statements that were used to take my children away. Angela, despite her apology, ultimately allowed herself to be used as a tool in their betrayal. This message confirms that Lance was not just a bystander, but was actively working behind the scenes to ensure I lost my children.

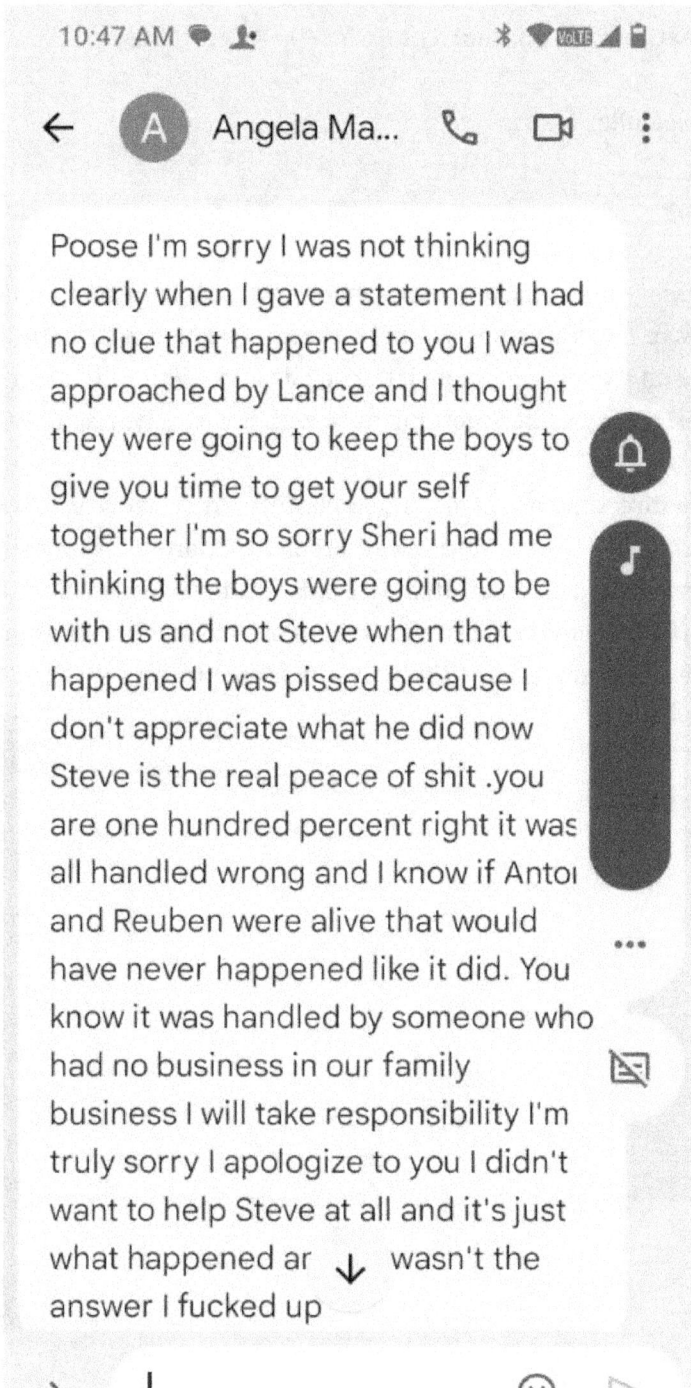

10:47 AM

A    Angela Ma...

Poose I'm sorry I was not thinking clearly when I gave a statement I had no clue that happened to you I was approached by Lance and I thought they were going to keep the boys to give you time to get your self together I'm so sorry Sheri had me thinking the boys were going to be with us and not Steve when that happened I was pissed because I don't appreciate what he did now Steve is the real peace of shit .you are one hundred percent right it was all handled wrong and I know if Antoi and Reuben were alive that would have never happened like it did. You know it was handled by someone who had no business in our family business I will take responsibility I'm truly sorry I apologize to you I didn't want to help Steve at all and it's just what happened ar ↓ wasn't the answer I fucked up

## Conversation with Sharon: The Cover-Up & Direct Lie

**Date: December 1, 2020**

**Summary:**

This message from Sharon is a blatant attempt to rewrite history and cover up the roles of Lance and Sheri in my betrayal. She insists that she and Angela were the only ones who wrote letters against me, while claiming that Lance and Sheri had absolutely nothing to do with it and only tried to help me.

This is a direct lie, as Angela's text confirms that Lance was the one who approached her to provide a false statement. Sharon's response is not just dishonest, it is a deliberate attempt to erase the involvement of the key players who worked together to destroy my life. This message serves as proof of how deep the deception runs, as she actively tries to protect Lance and Sheri from accountability.

🌐 100% 🔋

**Sharon** >

You didn't answer me. Why are you the only one footing the bill?

Never mind.

Sheri and I are paying for everything, whoever's wants to contribute is welcome but you know me I'm not begging anyone, people do what they want to do in life.

Here's the thing. He had burial insurance, but he had to use it to pay for the lawyer when you, Sheri, Angela and Lance helped Steven take my children away from me. See how Karma works.

Yes I do know how karma works and you are so wrong, angie and I were the only ones that wrote letters just because we knew you were not in anyway able to take care of them at that particular time. Sheri and lance had absolutely nothing to do with that. All they did was to help you.
.

# GLOSSARY

This glossary provides definitions of key terms related to narcissistic family dynamics and psychological abuse. These terms help explain the toxic behaviors and manipulative tactics described in this book.

**Communal Narcissist**

A communal narcissist gains admiration and control by presenting themselves as selfless, generous, and morally superior. Unlike the grandiose narcissist, who seeks attention through power and status, the communal narcissist seeks validation by portraying themselves as a "good person" who helps others. They are often active in charities, churches, and social causes, using these roles to manipulate and control people while maintaining a saintly public image.

**Covert Narcissist**

A hidden or "quiet" narcissist who does not display the grandiosity of an overt narcissist but is still just as manipulative and dangerous. Instead of being loud and arrogant, a covert narcissist plays the role of the victim, martyr, or misunderstood genius. They use passive-aggressive manipulation, guilt-tripping, and emotional blackmail to control others while appearing humble or innocent.

**Family Mobbing**

A form of group bullying within a family where multiple members gang up on a single target—the scapegoat. This can include spreading lies, isolating the victim, gaslighting, financial abuse, and character assassination. The goal is often to force the victim out of the family or make them doubt their own reality.

## Flying Monkey

A term used in narcissistic abuse to describe people who act on behalf of an abuser, carrying out their dirty work. Flying monkeys spread lies, manipulate others, and attack the victim to further the narcissist's control. They may be family members, friends, or enablers who are either deceived into helping or fully aware of their actions.

## Future Faking

A manipulation tactic used by narcissists and abusers to promise a better future that will never actually happen. It is designed to keep the victim hooked, hopeful, and emotionally invested in the relationship, preventing them from leaving. In romantic relationships, this could be a promise of marriage or commitment that never materializes. In family dynamics, the abuser might claim they will change and start treating the victim better, yet the abuse continues. In workplace settings, an employer may promise promotions or rewards that never come. Future faking creates false hope and keeps the victim stuck in the cycle of abuse, waiting for a future that will never come.

## Grandiose Narcissist

The classic, textbook narcissist—loud, arrogant, and obsessed with their own superiority. Grandiose narcissists believe they are smarter, better, and more important than everyone else. They demand constant attention, admiration, and praise. When their ego is threatened, they react with rage, entitlement, or revenge. Unlike covert narcissists, grandiose narcissists are easy to spot because they make their self-importance known to everyone around

**Gray Rock**

A strategy used to protect oneself from narcissistic individuals by showing no emotional response to their manipulative tactics. By acting uninterested and unengaged—like a "gray rock"—the person reduces the narcissist's interest in them, as narcissists thrive on eliciting reactions and controlling emotions. This technique involves keeping responses short, neutral, and unemotional, avoiding arguments or self-defense, responding with simple phrases like "I see" or "Okay," and not revealing personal thoughts or feelings that the narcissist can use against them. It is useful in family relationships, workplaces, co-parenting situations, and any interaction where going no-contact is not an control or

**Grooming**

A manipulative process used by abusers to gain trust, lower defenses, and pre-pare a victim for exploitation. Grooming can happen in families, relationships, workplaces, or communities. It often involves excessive praise or attention to build trust, testing boundaries with inappropriate jokes or small favors, isolating the victim from others, creating dependency (emotional, financial, or psychological), and gradually escalating control while making the victim feel complicit. Grooming is often associated with predatory behavior but can also occur in toxic relationships where an abuser conditions the victim to accept mistreatment.

**Hoovering**

A manipulative tactic used by narcissists or toxic individuals to "suck" someone back into a relationship or dynamic after a period of distance or no contact. This can involve flattery, guilt-tripping, love-bombing, false apologies, or even fabricated crises to regain control over their target. The term originates from the Hoover vacuum brand, symbolizing the way these individuals attempt to pull someone back into their influence.

## Love-Bombing

A manipulative tactic in which a person, often a narcissist or toxic individual, overwhelms their target with excessive affection, flattery, gifts, and attention to gain control or influence over them. This behavior creates an intense emotional bond, making the target more susceptible to manipulation. Once the target is emotionally invested, the love-bomber often shifts to devaluation or control tactics.

## Malignant Narcissist

The most dangerous and toxic type of narcissist. A malignant narcissist is a mix of narcissistic personality disorder (NPD) and antisocial personality disorder (ASPD). They are often cruel, sadistic, and enjoy the suffering of others. Unlike other narcissists, they don't just seek admiration—they seek control, dominance, and destruction. Malignant narcissists often engage in manipulation, lying, gaslighting, smear campaigns, and even criminal behavior.

## Narcissistic Injury

A term used to describe a narcissist's extreme reaction to criticism, perceived disrespect, or exposure of their true nature. When their false image is threatened, they respond with rage, revenge, or a smear campaign. They will do anything to protect their ego, even if it means destroying others.

## Scapegoat

The designated family outcast—the person blamed for everything that goes wrong. The scapegoat is often the one who sees the truth about the family dysfunction and refuses to stay silent. Instead of taking responsibility, the abusers deflect their shame onto the scapegoat, making them the target of ridicule, exclusion, and cruelty.

**Smear Campaign**

A deliberate and calculated attack on a person's reputation, usually carried out by a narcissist or their flying monkeys. The abuser spreads false stories, half-truths, and exaggerated claims to destroy the victim's credibility and isolate them from support. Smear campaigns are designed to turn others against the victim so the narcissist can maintain control.

**The Enabler**

The enabler is the person who supports, excuses, or covers up the abuser's actions. They may do this out of fear, denial, or a need for approval. In narcissistic family systems, the enabler defends the abuser, minimizes the abuse, and pressures others to stay silent. They often say things like, "That's just how they are," "You're too sensitive," or "You need to forgive and move on." Enablers keep the abuse going by protecting the abuser instead of the victim and play a critical role in maintaining the toxic family dynamic.

**The Golden Child**

The favored child in a dysfunctional family, often idealized and treated as superior. Golden children are often used as a tool to attack or undermine the scapegoat.

**The Lost Child**

The sibling who is ignored, overlooked, or emotionally neglected. Unlike the scapegoat or golden child, the lost child fades into the background.

**Triangulation**

A manipulative tactic where the abuser brings a third party into a conflict to control the situation, creating tension and division.

www.ingramcontent.com/pod-product-compliance
Lightning Source LLC
La Vergne TN
LVHW052034080426
835513LV00018B/2321